# Market Research in Travel and Tourism

For Alison and Sarah

# Market Research in Travel and Tourism

Paul Brunt

Butterworth-Heinemann

Linacre House, Jordan Hill, Oxford OX2 8DP
A division of Reed Educational and Professional Publishing Ltd

 A member of the Reed Elsevier plc group

OXFORD    BOSTON    JOHANNESBURG
MELBOURNE    NEW DELHI    SINGAPORE

First published 1997

**British Library Cataloguing in Publication Data**
Brunt, Paul
  Market research in travel and tourism
  1. Travel – Research   2. Tourist trade – Research
  I. Title
  910.6'88

ISBN 0 7506 3082 5

Printed in Great Britain by
Biddles Ltd, Guildford and King's Lynn

# Contents

# *Figures*

# Tables

# Preface

This book has grown out of my own teaching of research methods on undergraduate and postgraduate programmes and being involved in the development of several higher national diploma courses in tourism. It is intended primarily for undergraduate and final year HND students who are often faced with research projects or modules in this area. Many courses require students to undertake some sort of research investigation which requires primary data collection, designing questionnaires or conducting interviews. This book will provide some useful guidelines to help with this task.

There are eight chapters which begin by outlining the nature of research through market research in travel and tourism to how to plan a project. Chapters 4 to 6 give practical suggestions in terms of sampling, questionnaire design and data collection. Chapter 7 provides some background information regarding data analysis. It was never my intention to write a statistics text and hence this chapter explains only a small range of some of the most commonly used techniques. Additionally, many taught courses will involve training in computer software packages to analyse quantitative and, to a much lesser extent, qualitative data. It was felt to be beyond the scope of this book to provide another training manual for specific software. The final chapter shows how to write up research findings and give presentations, an area often under-valued in terms of its importance.

At the end of each chapter I have given some suggestions for selected further reading. My intention here was to provide a few key references to which the reader could turn  for more depth rather than to provide an extensive list of all possible sources.

Where appropriate I have added some exercises which, having read the chapter, the reader should be able to tackle. I have also included some case studies to illustrate further the issues raised in the chapter.

Doing research well can be stimulating and enjoyable and, in the field of travel and tourism, interesting too. Trial and triumph.

*Paul Brunt*

# *Acknowledgements*

The author extends thanks to those organizations which have given their permission to reproduce text: the British Tourist Authority and English Tourist Board, Central Statistical Office and Office of Population Censuses and Surveys (both now Office for National Statistics), and to P&O (UK) Limited. I am also grateful to my colleagues Derek Shepherd and Graham Busby for their advice and help.

# 1 *What is research?*

## Learning objectives

- Understand the main approaches to research.
- Appreciate the difference between market research and marketing research.
- Establish the role of market research in leisure and tourism planning and management.
- Identify some of the ethical considerations when undertaking surveys.
- Recognize some of the main tourism surveys.

## 1.1 What is research?

Research involves making a discovery about something previously unknown, and entails 'advancing human knowledge'. Undertaking research helps us to understand, explain or predict things that are of interest to us.

The types of research you are likely to come across can be viewed in three contexts:

1 **Scientific research** This is research that is conducted according to strict rules of logic and observation. A scientific approach is one where research is conducted in a systematic fashion. Normally this is associated with conducting experiments where, if researchers follow the same methods and techniques, they will gain the same results in their experiments. This aspect, often termed replication, is particularly important in scientific

research. Although the conditions of experiments may not always be replicated, scientists strive to achieve it to give weight to their conclusions.

2 **Social science research** Social science relates to the scientific study of society and social relationships. Social science is therefore much more about people and how they live. As people are often subjective and irrational, it is more difficult to carry out experiments in social science that are capable of being replicated.

3 **Applied research** Applied research uses the same methods and techniques of science or social science but the research is undertaken for a specific purpose that goes beyond solely advancing the body of human knowledge in the area. Therefore, applied research is designed to be put to a particular use.

Another way of classifying research is as follows:

1 **Pure research** This is mainly for academic interest alone. This is because, typically, the researcher chooses the topic of research with the aim of publication in academic journals and books. Alternatively, pure research is sometimes undertaken for higher degrees, such as doctorates. Whatever the circumstances, the aim of pure research is the advancement of knowledge in the area rather than an attempt to find an industry application.

2 **Action research** This is about combining academic understanding with industry application. Often the researcher undertakes work with a client or sponsoring establishment and both have agreed goals as to the outcomes from the research. Both parties have control of the research and agree necessary actions. The results may still be published by the researcher, perhaps with the support of the sponsoring establishment.

3 **Consultancy** This is research undertaken specifically for industrial or commercial purposes. The company or establishment sponsoring the research defines the problem and the researcher enters a contract as a consultant. The results are normally not published as they are very often commercially sensitive.

Beneath these types, all research can be further subdivided into:

1  Descriptive research        Finding things out to describe
                              /list/report
2  Explanatory research       Explaining things
3  Evaluative research        Combining the above to suggest
                              a course of action/make judge-
                              ments, etc.

Within the literature or company reports and the like it is very rare that the terms descriptive, explanatory or evaluative will be used to title a piece of research or a report. Nevertheless, all research is concerned with one or more of these categories.

## 1.2 Marketing or market research?

Research in marketing relates to the study of a market condition by methods which go beyond simply using factual information which arrives at the organization as a matter of course. In this context, the research is planned with thought given to the collection, analysis and presentation of data. The results of the research are then often used as an aid to management decisions. There is, however, some debate about what constitutes 'marketing research' as opposed to 'market research'. Holloway and Plant (1988) indicate that marketing research necessarily involves a wider variety of aspects, including research into new products, price, distribution channels, publicity and consumers. They argue that research into consumers and their patterns of behaviour can be more narrowly defined as market research.

This said, an executive who is about to conduct a research project either with company staff or through an agency, is likely to be less concerned as to whether the market research project is truly a subset of marketing research. Similarly the student on a professional tourism management programme facing an assignment is likely to be (rightly) more concerned to demonstrate rigour in the methods of data collection, application in the analysis and synthesis in the presentation.

Thus market research could range from talking quite informally to a few colleagues or clients to a highly formalized and complex series of multiple surveys, computer analysis of data and the construction of mathematical models to facilitate forecasting. In most cases, market research falls between these 'poles'.

## 1.3  Market research in tourism

Tourism is about people, their movement to destinations away from home and their activities on holidays. It is also about travel to and staying in places outside people's usual environment for business as well as leisure purposes. As such, research into tourism has its roots within the principles and practices of social science. Surveys are a way of collecting data for a variety of purposes and are used widely in the tourism industry, especially in collecting information about tourists and their activities. Students and researchers in search of information often find that it is only practical to gain information from groups of people rather than the whole population. For instance, a theme park might interview a sample of say 2000 visitors about their reactions to the park rather than all 300 000 visitors they get there in a year. Obviously to interview all the visitors would be impractical and costly, so researchers resort to what are called sample surveys. Surveys made on a smaller proportion of the population generally involve the use of questionnaires or interviews, and are based on the assumptions that:

- they contain within themselves, but on a smaller scale, the same characteristics,   relationships and processes of the larger group from which they come;
- they enable a consistent investigation of the group in question.

Within market research projects in tourism, surveys are common both within the industry itself and amongst researchers conducting projects of a more academic or 'pure' nature.

It is worth asking how market research in the travel and tourism industry differs from market research carried out in other industries. As Middleton (1994) suggests when discussing this issue in relation to the field of marketing, there 'appears to be common ground that the principles of the body of knowledge about marketing, and its main theoretical elements, can be applied in all industries and in commercial and non-profit sectors of the economy. Differences occur in the application of the theory.' This concept can also be applied to the more narrowly defined area of market research. The general theories, methods of data collection and analysis of market research are similar in all industries; however, when applied in this context they must be sensitive to the specific characteristics of the travel and tourism industry.

Smith (1989) provides a valuable insight into some of these particular characteristics in his book *Tourism Analysis*. Developing some of Smith's ideas it could be said that:

## 1 Tourism is a special type of human experience

Tourism is a particular type of human activity, and the purchase of a holiday is unlike the purchase of most other products. It requires the individual to give up their time as well as their money. How individuals reach their purchasing decisions in tourism is more complex than, for example, the purchase of a television, because so many more aspects are involved. Moreover many of these aspects are very difficult to measure as they are related to individuals' personal opinions, experiences and values.

## 2 Tourism is more strongly linked to advertising

Linking with the first point, it is often the case that an individual's awareness of a tourism product can be much lower than for other types of purchases. You cannot test drive a holiday nor send it back. Unless a holiday destination is well known through previous visits, the tourist is likely to be making a significant purchase of something completely untested. The role of advertising based on sound market research is, therefore, crucial for success.

## 3 The tourism industry is particularly vulnerable to outside forces

One aspect which distinguishes the tourism industry from many others is its vulnerability to outside forces. These range from political instability to changes in fashion. The favourability of a particular holiday destination can change quickly. The outbreak of a disease, rise in tourism related crime, acts of terrorism, swings in exchange rates or even a widely reported bad holiday experience – can drastically affect the level of business to that destination subsequently. While research can assist with some of these aspects, for example in estimating the political stability of an area, it is often the case that the tourism industry is highly susceptible to change as a result of outside forces.

#### 4 The tourism industry creates a variety of impacts

The economic, environmental, social and political impacts of tourism are well documented. As such, tourism may have a more widespread impact than many other industries. The need for market research information (alongside other forms of information) can help to clarify these impacts to enable planners and governments to reach appropriate decisions.

It can be seen, therefore, that a variety of factors begin to distinguish the nature of tourism and the tourism industry from other industries. When conducting market research in the field of travel and tourism these differences become apparent when traditional methods are applied.

## 1.4 Why are surveys useful in market research?

In a general context, Hoinville and Jowell (1978) state that 'systematic sample surveys can give more accurate measurements of a population's characteristics, attributes and behaviour than could be obtained by casual observation'. Further, Moser and Kalton (1993) conclude that, 'the value of surveys has been established beyond all question and in widely different fields'. These general comments are applicable to surveys in tourism in that such surveys are able to gain the facts about and the opinions of individuals who would perhaps be neglected by other methods. There are scientifically accepted principles governing the use of surveys to gain representative information about a larger population. Within tourism, surveys are useful for planning and management and marketing purposes. The use of surveys ranges from simple statements of a company's current position through to survey data which are analysed to predict future trends. Surveys are also used in the appraisal of the social benefits of tourism.

The managers of tourism operations require a thorough understanding of survey research methods to assist in the better management of areas such as planning, policy formulation and market research. Moreover, the tourism industry relies on a vast quantity of published statistics to assist in the financial management, marketing and forecasting of tourism enterprises.

Surveys can also assist as a public relations exercise. With a well designed questionnaire and trained interviewers, the respondent can be left with a positive feeling towards the company. Surveys can be used to help inform people about pending proposals or existing management strategies. Such factors have led to the wide-spread acceptance of surveys. Bardon and Harding (1981) stated that surveys 'will continue to be of major importance in recreation and tourism'.

Surveys are not without their problems and shortcomings. Problems exist if surveys are not designed properly with detailed attention given to each stage. Oppenheim (1966) was an early writer on this subject and stated that 'survey literature abounds with portentous conclusions based on faulty inferences from insufficient evidence wrongly assembled and misguidedly collected'. Despite this, as long as surveys use rigorous methods of design, data collection and analysis, they can be an invaluable tool. In this way surveys provide a context for better informed judgements and better directed decisions.

## 1.5 Ethical considerations

### Overview

Surveys are undertaken because of the need to know facts or opinions. However, the participants in surveys have rights to their individual privacy or even to be completely anonymous. People may wish to keep their feelings confidential and researchers need to be sensitive to these types of issue. The following is a list of aspects which should be considered to ensure that the rights of participants in surveys are reasonably dealt with.

### 1 Informed consent

The researcher should always inform potential participants in advance of any features of the research that might reasonably be expected to influence their willingness to take part in the study. Where the research topic is sensitive, the ethical protocol should include verbatim instructions for the informed consent procedure and consent should be obtained in writing.

Where children are concerned, informed consent may be obtained from teachers acting *in loco parentis*. However, where the topic of the research is sensitive, written informed consent should be obtained from individual parents.

## 2  Openness and honesty

So far as possible, researchers should be open and honest about the research, its purpose and application. Some types of research, for example in the area of social psychology, require deception in order to achieve their scientific purpose. Deception should only be approved in experimental procedures if the following conditions are met:

a deception is completely unavoidable if the purpose of the research is to be achieved;
b the research objective has strong scientific merit;
c any potential harm arising from the proposed deception can be effectively neutralized or reversed by the proposed debriefing procedures.

Failing to inform participants of the specific purpose of the study at the outset is not normally considered to be deception, provided that adequate informed consent and debriefing procedures are proposed.

## 3  Right to withdraw

All participants must have the right to withdraw from participation in the study at any time and must be clearly informed of this right at the outset. No attempt should be made by a researcher to persuade or coerce participants to remain in the study. In the case of children those acting *in loco parentis* should be informed of the right to withdraw the child from participation in the study.

## 4  Protection from harm

Researchers must endeavour to protect participants from physical and psychological harm at all times during an investigation. Where stressful or hazardous procedures are concerned, obtaining informed consent, whilst essential, does not absolve the researcher from responsibility for protecting the participant. In such cases the ethical protocol must specify the means by which the participant will be protected, for example, by the availability of qualified medical assistance.

## 5 Debriefing

Researchers must provide an account of the purpose of the study as well as its procedures. If this is not possible at the outset, then it should be provided on completion of the study.

## 6 Confidentiality

Except with the express written consent of the participant, researchers should be required to ensure confidentiality of the participant's identity throughout the conducting and reporting of the research. It may be necessary to specify procedures for how this will be achieved. For example, transcriptions of interviews may be encoded so that no written record of the participants' name and data exist side by side. Where records are held on computer, data protection legislation may apply.

## 7 Gender, race and culture

Procedures must always be sensitive to issues of race, gender, sexual orientation and disability. Researchers should respect the rights and sensitivities of religious groups and cultures of all kinds.

# Case studies: Some of the main tourism surveys explained

### 1 The British National Tourism Survey (BNTS)

The British National Tourism Survey (BNTS) is carried out every year by NOP for the British Tourist Authority and is summarized in a report called the *Digest of Tourism Statistics* (BTA, intermittently). The full report (four volumes) and access to a database is available for subscribers. The survey is carried out by means of personal interviews with a nationally representative random sample of adults (aged over 16) who are resident in Great Britain. Interviewing takes place in the November of each year and asks about holidays taken in the previous 12 months up to the 31 October. The BNTS is concerned only with holiday travel. A holiday is defined as being four nights or more away from home but information is additionally collected on all overseas travel of one or more nights. The fieldwork is carried out by NOP Travel and Leisure. The BNTS started in 1951 and has been conducted annually since 1960. Between 1985 and 1988 it was called the British Tourism Survey Yearly (BTS-Y).

Typically, approximately 3500 random in-home interviews of adults aged 16 years or over are undertaken in November/December each year. Occasionally this figure is increased by further interviews to raise the sample of holidays taken abroad to at least 2000.

## 2  The United Kingdom Tourism Survey (UKTS)

The United Kingdom Tourism Survey (UKTS) (English, Northern Ireland, Scottish and Welsh Tourist Boards, 1994) is a survey of tourism activities undertaken by adults and accompanying children within the UK. Included in this survey are trips to friends and relatives and travel for business as well as holidays which involve at least one night away from home. In addition to questions of purpose of travel and destination other results include method of transport, timing of holiday, length of stay, accommodation type, booking arrangements and leisure activities undertaken whilst away. The survey has been carried out each year since 1989 and is sponsored by the four national tourist boards, and results are published annually in a report called the 'UK Tourist'.

The survey method is face-to-face interviews in the respondent's home. For example, the 1993 survey involved 75843 interviews of people aged 15 years or older resulting in information on 22711 trips.

The sampling method is a two-stage stratified random sample (see Chapter 4). The first stage in developing a sampling frame involves dividing the whole country into 540 parliamentary constituencies in Great Britain and 24 wards in Northern Ireland. Within this, electoral registers are used to identify every fifteenth name on each register. Local interviewers then contact these individuals to request an interview.

The data from all interviews are weighted and grossed up to provide estimates both regionally and for the country as a whole. Like other surveys, this process involves a level of sampling error. The percentage error ranges from plus or minus 1.7 per cent for trips to all destinations to 12.9 per cent for trips within Northern Ireland.

## 3 General Household Survey (GHS)

The General Household Survey (GHS) is conducted by the Social Survey Division of the Office of Population Censuses and Surveys (OPCS, 1995). From April 1996 OPCS became part of the Office for National Statistics. The survey has been carried out annually since 1971, and since 1988 has been based on fieldwork for the preceding fiscal year. Thus the 1993 GHS is based on data collected between April 1993 and March 1994 and the results were published in 1995. A cross-section of people are interviewed in their homes. This cross-section represents respondents from differing geographic locations, housing types and socio-economic groups. For the 1993 GHS, interviews were conducted with 18 492 respondents, aged 16 or over, from 9852 households (OPCS, 1995).

The questions asked in the GHS are largely about social issues and changes. Every year questions are asked about employment, education, housing, health, fertility as well as the population characteristics. Occasionally additional topics are asked alongside these questions. In the area of leisure and tourism questions are asked every three to four years, as summarized below:

| Leisure and tourism questions | Year of GHS |
| --- | --- |
| Holidays (including length and countries visited) | 1973, 1977, 1980, 1983, 1986 |
| Leisure activities (including types and frequency) | 1973, 1977, 1980, 1983, 1986 |
| Sports activities (including frequency) | 1987, 1990, 1993 |
| Visits to heritage attractions | 1987 |
| Social activities and hobbies | 1973, 1977, 1980, 1983, 1986, 1987, 1990, 1993 |

Developed from OPCS (1995)

## 4 International Passenger Survey

The International Passenger Survey (IPS) is a survey of people travelling into and out of the UK (Central Statistical Office, 1995). A sample of travellers are interviewed using a face-to-face method of data collection. The IPS began in 1961 and since 1964 data have been continually collected. The UK Central Statistical Office

(CSO) commissions the work along with other government departments and the data collection and survey analysis is performed by the Office of Population Censuses and Surveys (OPCS). From April 1996 the CSO became part of the Office for National Statistics.

The results of the IPS are available in three formats. Monthly figures are produced in the 'CSO First Release' series *Overseas Travel and Tourism* published by CSO (Crown copyright 1995. Central Statistical Office. Published by HMSO). Quarterly results are available in the Business Monitor MQ6 titled *Overseas Travel and Tourism* produced by Her Majesty's Stationery Office. Annual data, with comparisons with previous years, are published by CSO in *Travel Trends*.

In the 1994 survey, 229 000 respondents were randomly selected for interview, representing approximately 0.2 per cent of all who were eligible. The principal questions asked concern nationality, residence, country of visit (UK residents travelling overseas), purpose of visit, flight or ferry information, earnings, expenditure and demographic characteristics. The survey has an 85 per cent response rate.

In terms of sampling (for further information see Chapter 4) a stratified random sample is used based on the seven principal airports, other regional airports, ferry ports and the Channel Tunnel. Different times and dates of interviewing are further stratified at each location over the survey period. The results are weighted and a complicated procedure of grossing up is carried out on the data.

As a large scale survey, the accuracy of the results is highly regarded by government and the tourism industry. That said, sampling error for particular countries varies. Some countries, such as France, have a very low level of sampling error because high numbers of people are travelling to and from that country. Others, such as Gibraltar, less frequently visited by UK residents and with fewer people from Gibraltar visiting the UK, have higher sampling errors.

## Summary

This chapter has introduced the main approaches to research in terms of the distinctions between pure research, action research and consultancy. The role of market research has been demonstrated to assist in the better marketing, planning and management of tourism facilities and enterprises. The focus of market research in tourism has shown that often the survey methodology is widely adopted. In addition, it is important that researchers in any field, including travel and tourism, must learn and follow certain ethical principles.

## Exercises

1 Explain the differences between scientific, social science and applied research.
2 Outline the principal distinctions between pure research and consultancy.
3 Review several textbooks on marketing and contrast the definitions of marketing research and market research.
4 Write some briefing notes for new interviewers which outline the ethical considerations necessary for a street survey on holiday behaviour.

## Further reading

Gill, J. and Johnson, P. (1991). *Research methods for managers.* London: Paul Chapman Publishing.

This is an excellent text covering the different approaches to research. The information includes the theory of research methods, research design and several chapters concerning the various problems involved with selecting an appropriate research strategy. Examples are taken from the general field of business and management studies.

Middleton, V.T.C. (1994). *Marketing in travel and tourism.* Oxford: Butterworth-Heinemann.

This book is divided into six parts and is a comprehensive text on all aspects of marketing. Part 1 has some useful sections which illustrate how marketing in travel and tourism is different from marketing in other industries.

Ryan, C. (1995). *Researching tourist satisfaction*. London: Routledge.

The first chapters of this book provide an overview of research methods and move into aspects of research design. Explanations are made with reference to the tourism industry.

Smith, S.L.J. (1989). *Tourism analysis: A handbook*. Harlow: Longman Scientific and Technical.

The first two chapters of this book are useful to appreciate the distinguishing features of tourism from other industries. In addition, Chapter 1 establishes the nature and scope of research into tourism in a wider context.

Veal, A.J. (1992). *Research methods for leisure and tourism*. London: Longman/ILAM.

The first chapters of this book outline the various approaches to research and show from where research in leisure and tourism originated. There is also a detailed discussion of cross-disciplinary approaches to research explained in a leisure and tourism context.

# 2    *Market research methods*

## Learning objectives

- Be able to distinguish between quantitative and qualitative approaches and to understand when it is appropriate to use them.
- Understand the range of methods of data collection commonly used in market research.
- Appreciate the pros and cons of different methods of data collection.

## 2.1  Quantitative or qualitative and primary or secondary

There has been a tremendous amount of literature about survey research methodologies. Often because survey research is multi-disciplinary there is disagreement over the best approach. Added to this, confusing jargon abounds; approaches to survey research may be inductive or deductive, descriptive or explanatory, experimental or non-experimental, positivist or interpretive. In short, whilst an awareness of some of these terms may be useful, often the survey problem dictates the approach and so the major decision that the researcher faces is over choice of method.

Here the choice is one of quantitative or qualitative and whether to go for primary data collection or secondary. These terms are now explained.

## Quantitative methods

These methods generally involve statistical analysis. This would mean that the results of studies using quantitative methods from perhaps a sample survey would be used to generalize about the survey population with a certain degree of confidence. Thus quantitative methods rely on numerical evidence to test hypotheses. Commonly to be sure of reliability in statistical tests large numbers of people (or units) would be interviewed and the information coded into numeric form and computers used to analyse the results. Quantitative methods can also be used on small numbers of people where the aim is not to generalize widely.

Some of the main attributes of quantitative approaches are:

1 identical questions and methods of recording the answers are used on each respondent so that the information can be recorded easily;
2 the sample is usually quite large and representative of the population under consideration;
3 statistical analysis is used to draw conclusions;
4 'closed' questions are used widely because they are more convenient for computer and statistical analysis;
5 attitudes and opinions are measured by the use of scoring and rating scales.

*Advantages of quantitative methods*

1 Large sample sizes commonly used are more representative of the population. Thus, statements about the population can be made to a degree of confidence.
2 Much information in the tourism industry is required in a quantitative form to enable managers to make decisions or to conduct meetings in an informed context.
3 Data are easily summarized and analysed using computers.

*Disadvantages of quantitative methods*

1 Quantitative methods are often more impersonal when compared to qualitative methods. Often a relatively small amount of information is known about people's life history or experiences.

2 Large samples are required to be representative of the population or to allow for statistical analysis.
3 Bias may be caused by poor questions or poor interviewers, which affects people's answers.
4 Samples may not always be representative because of the problems associated with those who decline to take part in a survey (how are they different from those who do take part?).

## Qualitative methods

These are research methods which give rise to non-quantitative information. In general terms this often means collecting a great deal of 'rich' information about relatively few people rather than more limited information about a large number of people. The techniques adopted include in-depth interviews, group interviews and participant observation.

Sometimes within the literature you may come across the term 'ethnography' (or ethnographic research/ethnographic fieldwork) in this context. Ethnography is a type of research which uses these techniques rather than being a single technique itself. The word *ethnos* derives from the Greek word meaning people, and therefore ethnography is about the study of people. The term has been stolen from anthropology – essentially the study of groups of people and, by a variety of qualitative methods, leading to an understanding of how a community works and what makes it 'tick'.

Some of the main attributes of qualitative approaches to data collection are:

1 The aim is to gain in-depth more open-ended answers rather than yes/no responses.
2 Usually the interviewer tries to get people to share their thoughts on a topic with the minimum of guidelines about how they should answer.

### *Advantages of qualitative methods*

1 'Rich' information is provided about people, their experiences, motivations, behaviour, their needs and aspirations.
2 Changes are encompassed over time.
3 They are more personal.
4 The information is understandable by the majority – statistical tests are less important.

*Disadvantages of qualitative methods*

1 Small numbers of people are normally involved, thus generalizations about the population at large cannot be made.
2 The measurement of qualitative material often requires judgements to be made by the researcher, hence questions of objectivity arise.

## Primary data collection

This relates to the collection of new information. This is the case where the researcher requires specific information which does not exist elsewhere or in another form. For instance, at recreation sites if information is required about how people regard the attractions, then it is only practical to ask them directly. It is, however, often sensible to consider whether it is worth going to the expense of collecting new information.

## Secondary data collection

This relates to the collection of data from sources which already exist. Thus the researcher is the secondary user. The use of census data, minutes of meetings or financial records are some sources of secondary information. In tourism the World Tourism Organization (WTO), Organisation for Economic Co-operation and Development (OECD), and the Economist Intelligence Unit (EIU) all publish invaluable sources of tourism data. Moreover, government departments and the British Tourist Authority, English, Welsh, Scottish and Northern Ireland Tourist Boards undertake surveys for a wide range of purposes which may provide valuable secondary information for the tourism researcher.

# 2.2  Survey methodologies – an overview

Below are some of the main methodologies used in the tourism surveys:

1   Observation methods
2   Literature review and sources of secondary data
3   Qualitative methods
4   Questionnaire based quantitative methods
5   Other methods

These are next described.

## 2.3 Observation methods

Observation is often a neglected technique but the results can be recorded both quantitatively or qualitatively (Veal, 1992). Some examples from tourism could include the use of informal leisure areas or the spatial use of sites in a field setting. Alternatively, consumer testing of equipment could be observed in a laboratory setting.

In tourism, much can be learned about human behaviour by observing it, even at a distance. For observation to be a reliable technique it must be systematically planned and relate to precise aims and objectives. One of the main difficulties associated with observation as a means of data collection is the amount of judgement that the researcher must apply. This is because:

- human behaviour is extremely complex;
- numerous factors affect human behaviour;
- only observing people may be erroneous;
- an amount of inference is required.

Despite these worries, observation can be a useful method of data collection. Sidney and Beatrice Webb (1932) were early researchers in this area and stated that 'an indispensable part of the study of any social institution, wherever this can be obtained, is deliberate and sustained personal observation ... from which the investigator may learn a lot. He clarifies his ideas ... revises his provisional classifications ... tests his hypotheses ... or even more importantly by watching committees etc., picks up hints that help him manifest new hypotheses.'

Thus, whilst it is perhaps unlikely that a whole research project will be based on observation methods alone, they are useful to:

- help gain a general understanding of the topic;
- help categorize different groups of tourists or types of behaviour;
- help test the project objectives;
- help develop new aims and objectives;
- provide data for analysis.

According to Nachmias and Nachmias (1981) there are three principal advantages of observation methods of data collection. Namely:

1 Directness. Behaviour is studied as it occurs. Instead of asking people what they do on holiday, for example, the researcher can observe it as it happens. This avoids the distortions which people may introduce when being asked to remember what they did.
2 Natural settings. Data are collected in the setting in which the behaviour or actions to be studied are taking place. Again this reduces the artificial elements that might intervene between an interviewer and respondent in a face-to-face interview. This is especially the case where those who are being observed are unaware that data are being collected.
3 Contextual background. The relationship between an individual and the environment in which they are, is perhaps best reflected in observational methods of data collection. To appreciate the atmosphere of a place is difficult, unless the researcher is actually there at the time.

## Types of observation

### 1 Unobtrusive observation

In some circumstances the use of cameras or one-way mirrors can be put to good effect to observe the activities of tourists. In airports for example, the queuing behaviour of people, as they check in, can be observed to make assessments of staff and tourists. In recent years the use of television cameras in tourist resorts has become common to help reduce crime. Alternatively, in the field, researchers can place themselves in suitable positions to watch the behaviour of tourists. For instance, tourists can be observed as they visit an attraction to gauge which are the most popular areas and to watch how people react to displays.

### 2 Participant observation

In this type of observation the researcher becomes part of the group he is researching and participates in the activities of the group. For example, the researcher becomes a tourist and feels the frustrations or enjoyments of other tourists in the group. This method can also be used to measure the efficiency of staff.

By being a customer in a restaurant or hotel the researcher can gain experience and get background material on how the staff function.

## Important considerations in observation methods

The main difficulty with methods of observation is the balance between subjectivity and objectivity. On the one hand data are collected which are rich, in that the observed may be unaware of the study and will therefore act naturally. On the other hand, the level of judgement that the observer has to introduce in the recording of the observation may bring into question the accuracy of the results.

In order to overcome or minimize these difficulties a systematic method of recording the observation is required. The level of control necessary to introduce into an observation study depends on the topic and the difficulty of judgement in the observations. One method would be to use an observation schedule where the observer records the actions of others according to definite pre-arranged plans. Often such schedules are the result of several pilot studies carried out to finalize the schedule. The development of an observation schedule can be complex and requires this trial and error if the data produced are to be reliable and, possibly, quantifiable.

An example of an early study was reported by Robert Bales (1950). His method of 'interaction process analysis' involved the systematic recording of the interaction of small groups of people. Within the group 'test persons' were observed to see how they reacted both verbally and non-verbally to different situations. In order to record their reactions, Bales developed an observation schedule of mutually exclusive categories:

1 Shows solidarity – raises others' status, gives help, reward.
2 Shows tension release – jokes, laughs, shows satisfaction.
3 Agrees – shows passive acceptance, understands, concurs, complies.
4 Gives suggestion – direction, implying autonomy for others.
5 Gives opinion – evaluation, analysis, expresses feeling, wish.
6 Gives orientation – information, repetition, confirmation.
7 Asks for orientation – information, repetition, confirmation.
8 Asks for opinion – evaluation, analysis, expression of feeling.
9 Asks for suggestion – direction, possible ways out.
10 Disagrees – shows passive rejection, formality, withholds help.

11   Shows tension – asks for help, withdraws out of field.
12   Shows antagonism – deflates others' status, defends or asserts self.

As you move through the categories, it can be seen that 1–3 are positive, 10–12 are negative and 4–9 are various categories relating to an essentially neutral position. Researchers would use this scale to record the reactions of the test persons as they faced different situations or discussions within their group.

## 2.4  Literature review and sources of secondary data

Virtually no research can be done without the benefit of references. Whatever the scale or nature of the project, the gathering of subject matter related to the topic is likely to be an important first and ongoing stage. Often for student projects a literature review is a specified requirement to demonstrate the student's awareness of the subject. When contemplating or undertaking a literature review, several points should be borne in mind (these have been developed from the ideas of Gill and Johnson (1991)):

1 Literature searches should take place early in the project, but should be ongoing to keep up to date with the latest articles from journals and magazines. However, do not become too bogged down in the literature as this can reduce creativity.
2 A literature review is a demanding exercise in its own right. The researcher needs to have an awareness of a wide range of information to be able to make sense of the field of enquiry. Can the subject area be categorized ? Perhaps there are general questions of concern to researchers in this field and secondary ones of more specific interest.
3 Whenever you start a literature review always keep records of what you have read. These will be required in the bibliography and may be required later when writing up. It is highly frustrating to be aware of a useful reference and not be able to locate it.

Clearly if information is already available which will answer the research questions posed, there is little point in collecting new information. Many organizations keep a variety of information or records which could be analysed. This type of data collection method refers to the collection of what is termed **secondary data**. Many companies find that the cost of collecting data at first hand (primary data) is such that managers need to consider whether data collected by others can be used for the purpose at hand. An example of historical research might be to use diaries, official documents or newspaper reports as sources. The official statistics compiled by government departments and public sector agencies provide a valuable source of information.

Secondary data can be analysed in a variety of ways depending on the nature of the project, but importantly, the object is to analyse them for a new or different purpose than for what they were originally collected. Additionally it should be borne in mind that the secondary data need not be quantitative.

## 2.5 Qualitative methods

This group of techniques I have put under the banner of qualitative as the purpose is more likely to:

1 develop hypotheses concerning behaviour or attitudes;
2 suggest methods for quantitative enquiry;
3 understand a decision-making process;
4 understand how people feel or react.

In addition, qualitative techniques can be a rigorous method of data collection in their own right. Some of the main methods include in-depth/informal interviews, focus groups and case studies.

### In-depth/informal interview

As a qualitative technique the in-depth interview with a respondent is designed to gather 'rich' information from a relatively small number of respondents rather than to statistically generalize from a large sample. In this latter case, this would be termed quantitative and become much more structured. Here, the in-depth interview has the following characteristics:

- The respondents discuss their experiences of something which is common to them. For example, particular groups of tourists or managers.
- Prior analysis of the subject has been undertaken by the researcher before the interview takes place.
- Question areas relating to the objectives of the research are asked, but then the respondents are at liberty to freely recount their experiences.

Often such interviews are tape recorded so that the content of the transcripts can be analysed following the interviews.

## Focus groups

These are similar in many respects to the in-depth interview but are conducted with a small group of people. This enables the interaction between the group to form an additional part of the data collection. Normally the researcher will act as the group leader and initiate the discussion. This aspect differs from observational methods where the researcher observes rather than takes an active part. Similarly the discussions of the group may be tape recorded or videotaped.

The group itself usually consists of up to ten people who have something in common with each other. For instance, they may all have stayed in a particular hotel. The atmosphere of the focus group is designed to be as relaxed as possible so that members feel at ease and are happy to recount their experiences.

## Case study

A case study is the intensive examination of an individual or small number of examples. The approach may involve techniques such as the scrutiny of secondary sources, in-depth interviews or focus groups. It can be considered as an opposite to large scale quantitative surveys (discussed in Section 2.6). For example, if a researcher was investigating holiday decision-making, he may choose to confine attention to an intensive study of a small number of families rather than a large sample survey. In the latter case the results would inevitably be more superficial. Thus case studies allow the researcher to 'get inside' the subject under study, but in doing so lose the opportunity for statistical generalizations.

Yin (1993) suggests that there are six different types of case study, as shown:

|  | Single case | Multiple case |
|---|---|---|
| Exploratory | 1 | 2 |
| Descriptive | 3 | 4 |
| Explanatory | 5 | 6 |

Single case studies focus on one individual, business or organization, whereas multiple case studies are of two or more. Exploratory case studies are concerned with developing research questions and objectives. Descriptive studies are about describing the case as a complete project, as in the case of a position statement. Explanatory case studies go further in attempting to explain the cause of the phenomenon within the case or cases under study.

## 2.6 Questionnaire based quantitative surveys

Questionnaire surveys are the most commonly used surveys in the tourism industry. They are used to gain information from people or respondents who answer questions about themselves, their knowledge of a particular subject and their opinions. The questions in the questionnaire are structured so that each respondent answers in exactly the same way. This enables the researcher to compare the answers of each respondent in a quantitative way. For example, pie charts and histograms can be constructed from the results to show the spread of answers to the questions.

There are two principal types of questionnaire survey relating to the method of data collection:

- Personal interviews
- Self-completion questionnaires

The difference relates to whether interviewers conduct the interview and complete the questionnaire on the respondents' behalf, or whether the respondents complete the questionnaire for themselves. These methods have different advantages and disadvantages which are discussed in the following sections.

1 The personal interview surveys (sometimes referred to as a face-to-face survey) can be sub-divided into three categories.
   a On-site
   b Home/office-based
   c Telephone interviews
2 Self-completion surveys, sometimes called postal surveys. (NB it is the self-completion aspect that is more important here. Drop and collect techniques, or putting under windscreen wiper are useful techniques used in this method, not just posting.)

## 1  Advantages/disadvantages of personal interview techniques generally.

**ADVANTAGES**
1 Personal contact with the respondent.
2 Verbal explanations can be given by interviewer as necessary.
3 Misunderstanding is reduced as the interviewer can gauge if respondent has understood the questions.
4 Avoids problems of limited literacy.
5 Unhelpful or inadequate replies can be probed.
6 Blanks (unanswered questions) are generally avoided.
7 Considerable amounts of detailed information can be collected by a trained interviewer.

**DISADVANTAGES**
1 Subject to interviewer bias.
2 Usually costly to implement.

### 1(a) On-site interviews

**ADVANTAGES**
1 Minimum time lag between questions about behaviour and opinions and the actual behaviour taking place.
2 Ensures users are contacted.
3 Response rates usually high – can be up to 95%.

**DISADVANTAGES**
1 Interviews have to be kept relatively short – normally less than 20 minutes.
2 As a consequence the range of questioning techniques is limited.
3 Can be difficult to carry out rigid sampling on complex sites.

## 1 (b) Home-based or office-based interviews

**ADVANTAGES**

1 Can be arranged at respondent's own convenience.
2 Interviews can be longer – up to an hour.
3 Wider range of questioning techniques can be used.
4 Includes non-users (for example, those who would not be selected by a site survey because they have not visited the site).
5 Sampling can be strictly controlled.
6 Response rates high – especially if prior contact/appointment made.

**DISADVANTAGES**

1 Time is involved in contacting each respondent.
2 Information about behaviour and opinions is retrospective.
3 May only include small number of users (as opposed to a site survey).

## 1 (c) Telephone interviews

**ADVANTAGES**

1 Reduces the costs involved in travel.
2 Answers can be easily computer coded as the interview progresses.
3 Sampling can be strictly controlled.

**DISADVANTAGES**

1 Rather anonymous, respondents may be less willing to recount experiences on the telephone.
2 Only involves respondents who have a telephone.

## 2 Self-completion techniques

**ADVANTAGES**

1 Large number of questionnaires can be distributed quickly and cheaply.
2 Training of staff need not be as intensive as for interviewing.
3 Respondents can complete questionnaire at leisure.
4 Removes possibility of interviewer bias.

**DISADVANTAGES**

1 Questions have to be simple and not open to misunderstanding.
2 No probing (further clarification) is possible.
3 The response rate tends to be lower (50 per cent is considered good).
4 Response rates can be variable – may get bias towards 'responsive' people.
5 Costs of distribution and postage.
6 There can be little control over when the questionnaire is completed.
7 The presentation of the questionnaire is important (more glossy to appear professional).
8 Failure to answer questions is more frequent and quality of answers can be variable.
9 Reminders often needed – costly and time consuming.

# Case studies

## Case study 1: P&O Cruises

P&O have been operating cruises for over 150 years, and currently offer over 60 cruises ranging from a three-day party cruise to a three-week trans-Pacific voyage. The company has three cruise liners, the *Canberra*, *Victoria* and the *Oriana*. In order to better understand their customers and to inform the company's marketing strategy, market research is undertaken on a regular basis. Two examples, using different methods of data collection, are explained below.

### (i)   Personal interviews

In 1994, P&O Cruises decided to use television advertising for the first time. The reason for this was related to the increase in capacity the company was able to offer with the launch of the *Oriana*. Thus, the company needed to attract more customers to its increased service. Television advertising was selected because of the better potential for communicating the experience of cruising over other means of advertising. It was felt that television could evoke a more emotional response which would overcome some of the more traditional objections to cruising. The objectives of the television campaign were to:

- generate a wider awareness of P&O cruises amongst the target audience;
- demonstrate the magical and dreamlike attraction of cruising;
- communicate the unique values involved in a P&O cruise;
- generate a powerful desire amongst the audience to try the product.

Alongside the television advertising campaign it was considered important to undertake market research to evaluate the effectiveness of this form of advertising. A market research agency was commissioned to carry out this research with the following objectives:

- to measure the impact of the campaign;
- to understand what the campaign communicates about P&O;
- to gauge the effect of the advertising on intention to purchase a cruise per se and a P&O cruise in particular;
- to establish key measures of brand health and track their movement in relation to advertising;
- to produce a competitive overview of cruise advertising/brands.

The methodology selected to address these objectives was personal, face-to-face interviews guided by a questionnaire. Because of the measurement over time that was required from the objectives, three periods of data collection were determined to be necessary. This was before, during and after the advertising campaign. In each period 300 respondents were interviewed nationally. The respondents were selected on criteria appropriate for this specific type of travel market, namely:

- they were over 40 years of age;
- they were in the A, B, C1 or C2 socio-economic groups;
- they did not reject the idea of cruising in the future;
- they had spent at least £750 per person on a holiday in the past or were willing to spend £750 per person on a cruise;
- they qualified in terms of their attitudes to and opinions of other types of products.

It can be seen that this method could be used to evaluate the effectiveness of the campaign as the method allowed the selection of particular respondents who could reasonably be assumed to be a potential customer for the company. Further, as the objectives required a level of measurement, this would suggest a quantitative approach for the main data collection. The number of interviews undertaken allows statistical analysis to help answer the research questions posed.

### (ii) Focus groups

With the introduction of the *Oriana*, P&O wanted to understand how the *Oriana* was currently positioned in consumers' minds with regard to other cruise ships generally and other P&O ships specifically. To establish this, focus groups of current *Oriana* passengers were selected to discuss the reactions and opinions with the following objectives:

- to establish how consumers are drawn to an *Oriana* cruise;
- to evaluate how the *Oriana* is perceived against the *Canberra* and *Victoria*;
- to assess the gap between the expectations and the reality of an *Oriana* cruise;
- to evaluate the effect of *Oriana* on P&O Cruises corporate brand image;
- to establish the intention of *Oriana* cruisers to cruise again.

Seventy-two *Oriana* passengers were selected in terms of their residence in Britain (North and South division) and a twofold measure of socio-economic circumstances. In addition, groups were divided in terms of whether the respondents were loyal P&O customers, new to cruising, or competitive customers (used other companies as well). This resulted in six categories of respondent, and two focus groups of six respondents were conducted for each category. The focus group sessions lasted approximately one-and-a-half hours. With these objectives, which are more exploratory in nature than the previous example, a qualitative approach is more suitable.

### Case study 2: British Coach Operators Survey

By 1990, it was estimated that there were some 5000 coach operators in Britain (British Tourist Authority and English Tourist Board, 1990) but little was known about their structure, composition or how involved coach operators were in the UK domestic tourism market. The English, Welsh and Scottish Tourist Boards commissioned a research agency to provide information on the coach industry's involvement in domestic tourism and to establish a database of the most active operators. Further, more specific, objectives were also defined.

Given the lack of information, a two-stage approach was adopted. The first stage was essentially exploratory and 15 in-depth interviews with operators were undertaken nationally to provide qualitative information. The results of these interviews enabled a second, quantitative stage to take place. During this stage 385 coach operators were interviewed by telephone. Operators were randomly selected from a list drawn from various directories, and again this reflected national coverage.

As mentioned earlier in this chapter, this example can be seen as a typical case of where exploratory qualitative methods are used as an aid to develop a subsequent quantitative stage. Without the 'rich' information provided by the in-depth interviews, and in the absence of relevant secondary data, a quantitative survey alone may have easily failed to satisfy the objectives. In-depth interviews help the researcher develop an understanding for the subject, which can then be used to develop a quantitative survey in an informed way.

## Case Study 3: Leisure Day Visits Survey

In 1991, the Social Survey Division of the Office of Population Censuses and Surveys (OPCS) reported on a survey of leisure day trips in Great Britain in 1988/89 (OPCS, 1991). The work had been carried out on behalf of the then Employment Department and the British Tourist Authority/English Tourist Board. The aim of the survey was to find out information about the volume and day trip behaviour. Day trips were defined as a journey away from home lasting at least three hours but less than 24 hours for recreational purposes (some exclusions were given in the definition, for example, journeys to work). It was decided to collect the data by using an additional questionnaire alongside the General Household Survey (GHS) (see case studies in Chapter 1). As previously mentioned, the GHS adopts a personal interview method in the respondent's home.

Before selecting the interview method, a diary method of data collection was tested to assess which of the two methods would be best for the purposes of this survey. Tests were carried out to see how the two methods performed against each other over a variety of criteria. These are summarized in Table 2.1.

It was perhaps the last point in Table 2.1 which swayed the decision to select interviews over diaries. For instance, where there was more than one reason why a day trip had been undertaken, respondents alone were unsure how to record it in the diaries. In interviews probing is possible with trained interviewers able to get full and developed answers from respondents. It should be remembered however that diary methods of data collection can be valuable where the information to be recorded is straightforward. Here the advantages of the method in terms of recall can be used to best effect.

## Summary

The survey methodology is perhaps the most important method of data collection in travel and tourism research. It is used widely by both academics and commercial organizations alike. Government departments and the public sector side of the tourism industry also use surveys to enable informed judgements to be made.

When conducting a survey, the method of data collection is crucial to the overall success of the project. Awareness of the pros and cons of each of the methods is important when decisions are to be made on the results of the research. The reliance on a single method of data collection is unlikely to ever be an ideal approach.

## Exercises

1 For the following methods of data collection, give a definition and suggest a suitable research project in travel and tourism where you might expect each method to be used.
   - In-depth interview
   - Focus groups
   - Personal interview
   - Site survey
   - Telephone survey
   - Postal survey
2 What is the principal difference between qualitative and quantitative research?
3 Defend the need for observational methods of data collection in travel and tourism research.

**Table 2.1** *Comparison of methods in the Leisure Day Visits Survey*

| | Diary | Interview |
|---|---|---|
| Method | Diary left with one respondent per household to record details of day trips taken by the household over a four week period. Diaries collected. | Retrospective interview with one respondent per household requiring the same information on day trips for the household. |
| Response rates | This was found to be 68%. | 79% was achievable. |
| Quality of information recalled | There was a satisfactory recall over the four-week period. | The maximum period of recall for information to be properly remembered was two weeks. |
| Cost | The two methods were largely equivalent in terms of cost. If diaries were posted back (rather than collected) then costs were reduced but response rates were considerably lowered. | |
| Questions | These had to be simple as no interviewer was present to assist. | More complex questioning was possible. |

Developed from OPCS (1991)

# Further reading

## 1 General texts

Fowler, F.J. (1993). *Survey research methods*. Second edition. London: Sage Publications.

This is a general text on survey methods with the fourth chapter devoted to identifying different methods of data collection.

Moser, Sir C.A. and Kalton, G. (1993). *Survey methods in social investigation*. Second edition. London: Heinemann.

The first edition of this book, written by Moser, was published in 1958. Since then the book has been updated and reprinted many times. It was perhaps the first book to be published covering the whole field of survey techniques. There are several chapters which focus on data collection methods which include observation, using secondary sources, as well as collecting information where questionnaires are used.

Frankfort-Nachmias, C. and Nachmias, D. (1992). *Research methods in the social sciences*. Fourth edition. London: Edward Arnold.

This book in its fourth edition covers a wide range of topics in this area. Four chapters are devoted to methods of data collection which include reference to observation methods.

## 2  Texts on particular methods of data collection

Yin, R.K. (1993). *Applications of case study research*. London: Sage Publications.

This book is divided into three parts. The first part introduces the theory of the case study approach before, in the second part, giving examples (from an educational and management background) of the case study method with reference to important considerations when using this procedure. The third section examines the use of case studies in evaluative research and demonstrates how the case study approach differs from other qualitative strategies.

Lavrakas, P.J. (1993). *Telephone survey methods: Sampling, selection and supervision*. London: Sage Publications.

Introduces telephone surveys as a particular method of data collection. This is developed to investigate telephone sampling methods, techniques of securing cooperation and how to supervise telephone interviewers.

Krueger, R.A. (1994). *Focus groups*. Second edition. London: Sage Publications.

This book is divided into three parts. The first is a detailed explanation of the nature of focus groups. The second explores how to plan, run, ask questions, analyse results and report on the findings of focus groups. The final part deals with special audiences, difficult situations that may be encountered and how to contract in specialists to run focus groups.

Stewart, D.W. and Kamins, M.A. (1993). *Secondary research: Information, sources and methods*. Second edition. London: Sage Publications.

Explains the nature of secondary data collection and evaluates how and when this method is possible and appropriate. The authors provide guides to accessing United States Government Census data, other government sources, non-government sources and CD-ROM technology. In addition, other sections include how to use and integrate secondary information into research projects.

| 3 | *Planning a project* |
|---|---|

## Learning objectives

- To outline how you would go about planning and preparing a market research or consultancy project.
- To understand the various stages in the planning process.
- To appreciate the need to modify the planning stages for different types of project.

## 3.1 Why is it being done?

When contemplating developing a market research project it is important to recognize why the project is being undertaken. This may seem to be an unnecessary question, but a request for information about a market may reach the researcher from a variety of sources within a company and the amount of work involved can similarly be varied. For a research budget to be justifiably allocated there must be initial confidence in the validity of the research that has been requested.

As an example, consider that a tour operator has developed a completely new type of package holiday. A survey of current customers is proposed to assess what effects this new market will have on the business. In this instance, will such a survey yield useful results? The existing customer base is easy to tap into, names, addresses and some buying characteristics already exist on the company's database. A simple self-completion questionnaire could easily be sent out with a prize holiday offered as an inducement to return the questionnaire. Moreover, in the past, existing customers have indicated what they like and dislike about the company's products. Their views have been incorporated wherever possible and the company has maintained a competitive edge. But how can past customers react to a new type of product which they have yet to experience? What objective statements would they be able to make? Whilst the tour operator may be convinced of the superiority of this new product will this inevitably lead to success?

In such a situation it is unrealistic to expect that the results of a market research exercise will provide all the answers. Some indications may come to light but it is doubtful that an estimate of how much market share this new product will capture can be predicted with certain accuracy.

Another situation which occasionally arises is that market research is carried out when the organization is in a crisis. Market research should be an aid to management decisions and not an undertaking that will, alone, determine policy. As Livingstone (1977) suggests, it is 'not unknown for a market research agency to be called in almost as an act of death-bed repentance and be expected to guarantee salvation.' In this sense, it should be remembered that market research does not exempt management decision-making or the recruitment of an outside troubleshooter to make the unpleasant decisions that none among the senior executive want to make.

## 3.2 An overview of the planning stages

There are a wide variety of models suggested by authors regarding the stages of a research project. Veal (1992) identifies 17 preparatory stages, four investigatory stages, four analysis stages and three write-up steps. However, he and others acknowledge that each project may require a different approach. Pure, academic research is clearly distinct from a consultancy contract where objectives may be solely determined by the client. The following overview represents a synthesis of various sources together with the author's own experiences.

### Planning a research project

Stage 1   Definition of the problem and development of research questions.

Stage 2   Identification of information needs, to include:

> – literature review;
> – review of secondary sources;
> – primary data requirements;
> – data collection methods;
> – sampling frame;
> – fieldwork arrangements;
> – analysis requirements;
> – budget implications.

Stage 3    Redefinition of the problem, the question and information needs (often in the light of budget and time constraints)

Stage 4    Statement of aims and objectives

Stage 5    Development of a research programme

Stage 6    The pilot stage

Stage 7    Data collection

Stage 8    Data coding and analysis

Stage 9    Report and presentation preparation

Each of these stages will now be investigated in more detail.

## 3.3  The stages explained

### Stage 1  Definition of the problem and developing research questions

It must be assumed that market research has been determined as necessary, as suggested in the first section of this chapter. The definition of the problem may require considerable negotiation between the researcher and whoever is commissioning the research. Time spent on this stage avoids awkward comments in the final presentation such as 'we knew that' or (even worse) 'that wasn't what we wanted'. Such comments cannot always be considered the sole fault of the researcher.

At the outset of planning market research the researcher should begin by familiarizing themselves with the topic of the enquiry. The likelihood is that this will involve finding out what has been done before in the same or similar topic areas. In the case of academic or pure research the project may have come about from the researcher's own interests. Alternatively in action research or consultancy the researcher may be given the project as part of his/her normal job or as a consultancy contract. In this latter case there are often briefing meetings between the employer/client and employee/consultant. The purpose of these meetings is shown in Table 3.1.

**Table 3.1**  The purpose of briefing meetings

|  | *Aims* |
| --- | --- |
| Employer/client | To ensure research is successfully completed, and to recruit a suitable researcher. |
| Employee/ consultant/ researcher | To gain full understanding of project requirements and to convince employer that they are suitable and competent. |

Thus the researcher must now learn something of the subject and ask questions in the briefing meeting that lead to a thorough understanding of the project requirements on both sides. The researcher must know what is required and assure the commissioner about being the right person for the task. In the area of consultancy, familiarization with the subject is essential because whilst the consultant will be experienced in terms of the methods of market research he or she may have limited experience of the subject of the enquiry. Pertinent questions in briefing meetings also enable the researcher to establish whether there is a 'hidden agenda' at play. Is the market research being used to disguise and facilitate a particular course of action that has already been determined?

An example of the type of thinking necessary at this stage (and throughout the initial stages) will be developed in the following hypothetical example.

### Holiday Farms Cooperative

*A group of 100 farmers offering farmhouse bed and breakfast (B+B) accommodation have been working as a cooperative for the last ten years. Each farmer pays an annual subscription to an executive committee elected by the members. The level of subscription is related to the size and nature of the accommodation and is allocated to a marketing fund. This fund allows for the production of a simple brochure which is distributed to tourist information centres and town libraries. Occasional coverage is provided by the local authority public relations section in the press and at certain travel shows and exhibitions. The co-operative has been successful in developing and maintaining a satisfactory level of business to the members over the last ten years. Whilst most visitors book their accommodation directly, they have recently introduced a referral service operated by one of the members. There have, however, been fluctuations in profitability and occupancy rates and the executive committee have decided to commission a researcher to evaluate whether the limited marketing budget is being spent in the most effective way.*

*Initially, to gain an understanding of the topic the researcher might need to establish:*

- *What is the size of the B+B market in the local area, regionally and nationally?*
- *How has this market developed in recent years?*
- *Does it appear to have growth potential or is it declining?*
- *Who or what is the competition?*
- *What are the nature and prices of the accommodation?*
- *Who are the customers and what are their opinions of the service provided?*

*The researcher might informally interview some of the members, as well as looking into statistical sources produced regionally and nationally. Following this negotiations can progress with the executive committee to better establish what is actually required of the researcher.*

After initial work in defining the problem it should be possible to develop some research questions. That is to turn the initial statements or topics into the form of questions. In the case study this might conceivably include:

*From* _____

*To develop a marketing strategy for the Holiday Farms Cooperative.*

*To* _____

1 *Determine the nature/types of accommodation within the cooperative and the types of visitor they attract.*
2 *To establish which types of accommodation have been more successful than others and why.*
3 *To investigate options for the distribution of brochures.*

4 *To evaluate the national market for farmhouse B+B and the cooperative's position in it.*
5 *From the analysis of 1–4, investigate how the marketing budget can best be spent.*

Hence, the general statement has begun to be broken down into smaller, more achievable, parts or research questions.

## Stage 2 Identification of information needs

The second stage of the project plan overlaps with the first in as much as the definition of the problem will inevitably involve some identification of material that will be used in the later stages. However, what distinguishes this stage of the project is the move away from 'what is the project about' to 'how might it be carried out'. Depending on the nature of the project there are several aspects which would receive some consideration.

### (a) Literature review

As already mentioned in Chapter 2, a review of relevant literature is an essential stage. The research may gain ideas about the sorts of question which should be addressed or tips on successful methods of data collection and analysis. Similarly, ideas about how a report could be organized can be usefully gained by looking at the work of others.

A literature review would involve reading articles in magazines and trade journals, newspapers as well as books. When scanning an article it is always worthwhile to see to whom the author has referred and follow up these references. Many larger public libraries and academic libraries have computerized index systems which can collate references under a key word search. However, if words such as 'travel' and 'tourism' were searched for, the researcher may be lost under the mountain of paper of references under these general headings.

In addition to works published by authors writing about the topic or their own research findings, other types of sources may provide valuable tips. Examples of brochures or other forms of printed information could be investigated. This is developed further with the case study.

*Holiday Farms Cooperative: literature search*

*Sources investigated include articles from journals such as:*

*Annals of Tourism Research*
*Articles in Hospitality and Tourism*
*HCIMA current awareness bulletin for Hospitality Management*
*Holiday Which*
*Hospitality*
*International Journal of Contemporary Hospitality Management*
*International Journal of Hospitality Management*
*International Tourism Quarterly*
*International Tourism Reports*
*Journal of Contemporary Hospitality Management*
*Journal of Travel Research*
*Leisure, Recreation and Tourism Abstracts*
*Tourism Management*
*Travel and Tourism Analyst*
*Worldwide Hospitality and Tourism Trends (CD-ROM)*

*For all of these sources back issues would be scoured for anything on the same or similar topics. In addition, brochures from the main competitors both nationally and locally would be gathered to compare different approaches.*

### (b)  Secondary sources of data

The difference between items in a literature review and sources of secondary data relate to how the information will be used. As previously explained, the purpose of the literature review is to gain knowledge of the subject, pick up tips and perhaps use references in a report to help justify or compare. Secondary sources of data form part of the actual data collection. The 'secondary' element indicates that the data have already been collected for another purpose. Sources of secondary data can be categorized in a number of ways; one example follows.

**INTERNAL SECONDARY SOURCES**

These are sources of data available from within an organization. They include:

- minutes of meetings;
- reports from sales representatives and the like;
- financial records;
- internal reports.

## EXTERNAL SECONDARY SOURCES

There are a variety of external sources of secondary data which can be further sub-divided:

### (I) OFFICIAL STATISTICS

Government departments and other public sector agencies undertake surveys for all sorts of purposes. In the tourism field some of the main examples include:

- Tourism Intelligence Quarterly;
- Business Monitors MA6 and MQ6;
- Business Travel News;
- British Tourist Authority, Digest of Tourism Statistics;
- Social Trends;
- British National Travel Survey;
- UK Tourism Survey;
- Control of Immigration Statistics;
- Sightseeing in England;
- Holiday Intentions Survey;
- Survey Among Visitors to London;
- Occupancy Surveys in England, Scotland, Wales and Northern Ireland.

The above is a small part of the wide variety of official statistics available, occasionally free of charge. In addition, international sources of statistical information are available from organizations such as the World Tourism Organization (WTO) and the Organisation for Economic Co-operation and Development (OECD).

### (II) COMMERCIAL SOURCES

There are some commercial organizations who undertake surveys which researchers can subscribe to or purchase reports from. Organizations which do this sort of work include Mintel, the

Economist Intelligence Unit (EIU), Eurostat, Tourism Planning and Research Associates and Business Strategies Ltd. As an example Business Strategies Ltd produced a report entitled 'Tourism: The deliverables' (1995), which researchers can purchase for £4250 +VAT. The use of this type of information depends on the nature of the project and it is always wise to consider what was the purpose behind the collection of the data originally.

### Holiday Farms Cooperative : secondary sources

*Internal sources include the occupancy rates of all members since joining the cooperative, executive committee minutes, prices and accommodation details. Some limited information exists on the origins of visitors. External sources include the regional tourist board's factsheets which indicate the ranges of accommodation and occupancy rates for all types of accommodation in the region. Other national surveys (BNTS and UKTS) are available showing trends in visitors and the popularity of farmhouse B&B.*

### (c)  Primary data requirements

Having scoured the literature and become aware of the range of secondary data sources available, the next decision is to consider what will still have to be found out. Thus remaining gaps will require specific methods of data collection for the purpose of the research project.

### Holiday Farms Cooperative : primary data

Whilst some secondary sources of information can be used, nothing exists regarding visitors' decision-making to select accommodation, their satisfaction from it or their socio-demographic characteristics. To inform the marketing strategy, this information will require primary data collection.

### (d)  Data collection methods

Once the necessity of primary data has been established, the methods of data collection require consideration. As outlined in Chapter 2, a decision will have to be made as to a quantitative or qualitative approach, or a mixture of both. The pros and cons of the individual methods will have to be evaluated and limitations recognized. Unfortunately, there is often no right or wrong answer in the selection but time and financial constraints may often be a determining factor. Clearly the nature of the project in terms of the level of precision required from the results will have a significant bearing on the methods of data collection. What is required from descriptive research (such as in a position statement) is different from the methods needed to facilitate financial forecasting.

### Holiday Farms Cooperative : data collection methods

To establish primary information on the customer base, a self-completion questionnaire could be constructed and distributed to all visitors by the owners. This would provide essentially quantitative information about the visitors and their opinions. To supplement this, a series of in-depth personal interviews could be carried out with a sample of visitors to provide qualitative information supporting the quantitative information on attitudes and opinions.

### (e)  Sampling frame

This aspect will be discussed more fully in Chapter 4. At this stage in the planning process, decisions need to be made regarding how many people to interview, where and when to interview, and the length of the survey period. Again the nature of the survey will determine sample size, for example, as well as the expected response rate for the data collection method and available resources.

### Holiday Farms Cooperative: sampling frame

*An initial estimate on past records suggests that there is a 35 per cent occupancy rate, resulting in approximately 3500 visitors to the 100 farmhouses. For a self-completion questionnaire distributed and collected by the owners, a response rate of 50 per cent would be considered good. If an attempt was made to leave a questionnaire in visitors' rooms this might yield 1750 responses. However, even allowing for errors and a lower response rate, over 1000 questionnaires are likely to be produced by this method. For quantitative comparisons to be made, and given the differing types of accommodation and occupancy rate within the cooperative, this is deemed adequate. For the qualitative survey 50 in-depth personal interviews covering a range of times and types of farmhouse is considered sufficient to provide a wide range of detailed information.*

### (f)  Fieldwork arrangements

Depending upon the nature of the project and the methods of data collection selected, there will be a variety of fieldwork to organize. At this stage in the planning process it is a case of preliminary identification of what will be required. This may well include:

- arranging permission to interview at a site;
- getting access to names and addresses of potential respondents;
- getting quotes for the printing of questionnaires, etc.;
- establishing the training requirements of staff, or the need for the recruitment of staff.

### Holiday Farms Cooperative : fieldwork arrangements

*Permission to involve the members of the cooperative is implicit in the project. At this stage consideration would be given to arranging a workshop on the distribution and collection of the self-completion questionnaire. For the qualitative interviews, this would require a trained interviewer. Identification of a suitable person would be necessary if the researcher was not going to conduct the interviews. Clerical assistance may be required in the coding of questionnaires and transcription of the interviews.*

### (g)  Analysis requirements

Before any data are collected it is worth considering how the data will be analysed in terms of what computer package will be used and what statistical techniques will be applied. At this stage it is necessary to reflect on how the research questions posed might be answered when analysing the data. If this is in part by means of statistics, consideration should be given to any particular requirements of the proposed statistical test. Some tests require a minimum number of responses to be reliable.

### Holiday Farms Cooperative: analysis requirements

*The quantitative survey will use statistical techniques to determine the socio-demographic characteristics of the respondents and their opinions of the accommodation. Independent variables such as place of residence, age, type of group, social class and previous experience will be used to cross-tabulate against dependent variables such as the respondents' rating of quality, satisfaction and likelihood of repeat purchase. The chi-square test will be used to establish the significance of the variables (this is more fully explained in Chapter 7). The likely response rate is sufficiently large for variation amongst the respondents to be established by this technique. The qualitative interviews will be analysed in terms of the content of the transcripts, and areas of contradiction and agreement will be investigated.*

### (h) Budget implications

It is highly unlikely that financial implications have not already been considered by this point in the planning process. For 'in-house' surveys, as in action research, a budget may have been pre-determined and the researcher has borne this in mind in the early planning stages. With consultancy contracts some clients outline a maximum budget in their brief. However, other contracts do not stipulate any budget guidelines and in preparing a tender document the consultant may have to weigh up several aspects. This often involves trying to anticipate what the client may be willing to pay. The consultant must be convinced that the methods proposed are appropriate and achievable and then has to charge accordingly. Cheaper budgets suggesting inferior methods may not necessarily win the contract.

## Stage 3 Redefinition of the problem

This is perhaps one of the most awkward stages in the research process. The researcher has attended briefing meetings, undertaken some literature searches, identified a range of secondary data sources, thought about the primary data requirements, methods of data collection, fieldwork, analysis and prepared a budget. In action research the researcher may then be required to submit the proposal to a committee or senior management. For consultants this may be presented to the client as a tender document. Whichever is the case, this initial work may disappear for some time before being returned to the researcher. The possible outcomes at this stage may well include the following:

1  Everything is fine and the research may progress.
2  Further clarification is requested.
3  The project is too costly or no longer needed and is dropped.
4  The consultant is unsuccessful and the contract has been awarded elsewhere.
5  A less expensive or different option is decided upon, perhaps concentrating on the secondary sources alone or a smaller sample size.

Clearly points 3 and 4 are the researcher/consultants' nightmare. In the case of point 4 it is very unusual for the consultant to be able to charge for the work completed to this point. In the case of the action researcher point 3 it can be just as disappointing in the wasted effort but may reflect a change in policy (hopefully) rather than inadequacy on the part of the researcher.

Points 2 and 5, requiring clarification or modification, are common outcomes and therefore require a process of redefinition before the project is agreed. The danger here, though, is that delays may ultimately result in the postponement because of missing, or not being prepared for, the survey period. In surveys of a travel and tourism nature there may be a precise season when data collection must take place, otherwise few tourists are available for interview.

## Stage 4  Statement of aims and objectives

Following any necessary changes and redefinition the project is ready to begin. At this point it may be useful to reiterate the aims and objectives. With consultancy contracts these may have been unchanged from the original brief. The crucial point is that both the researcher and whoever is commissioning the research are clear about what is required from the project in terms of its aims and objectives.

## Stage 5  Develop a research programme

The preliminary work of stage 2, if largely unchanged, will be developed in this stage. This entails:

1  Further reviews of literature.
2  Acquisition of secondary sources.
3  Confirmation of primary data requirements and methods of data collection.
4  The development of a sampling frame.

5 The design of questionnaires and observation recording sheets (if appropriate).
6 Specification of the fieldwork arrangements.
7 Specification of the analysis requirements.

In some cases a proposed questionnaire may have had to be included in the tender proposal at an earlier stage. Overall, this stage represents the tidying of loose ends before the project starts to 'roll'.

## Stage 6  The pilot stage

Having designed the necessary questionnaires, it is vital to test them out before the final launch into the data collection. The researcher, having put such effort into the project to date, may easily believe that the whole world is as interested in the topic as he/she has become. It is then easy to lose sight of how respondents will react and what level of understanding they might have. Therefore it is necessary to see how things might work out. Thus questionnaires, interviews or observations should be carried out on a small number of potential respondents first. This is called a pilot survey, which highlights:

- problems with questionnaires (wording, layout etc.) causing misunderstanding;
- problems with interviewers who are not fully conversant with their requirements;
- an indication of the likely response rate;
- an indication of the range of responses to the questions which can be suggestive of the likely results.

From the pilot survey, modifications may have to be made and re-tested if necessary. If there are few or no changes to be made, it may be tempting to include the results of the pilot survey within the main data collection. However, before this dangerous course of action is undertaken, consideration should be given to what effects this extension of the survey period (to include the pilot stage) might have. Moreover, what differences might the respondents of the pilot have against respondents of the main survey? Were they contacted by interviewers in the same way as is planned for the respondents in the main survey? Few authors comment on this point, perhaps assuming that the results of the pilot will affect the main survey in such a way that inclusion of pilot data is never contemplated. In the opinion of this author, this practice is setting a dangerous precedent. Having set out with a research programme geared to the successful completion of the project, to change it in this way now appears unscrupulous.

## Stage 7  The data collection

This stage is either dreaded most or comes as a welcome relief. All the planning has been completed and the survey begins. With personal interviews the project begins to 'run itself' in terms of actually doing the fieldwork and travel to the site or people's homes. With postal, self-completion questionnaires there can be a brief lull in the proceedings. Having posted all the questionnaires there is often perhaps a week before they start being returned.

Whilst the data collection is underway, there is much that the researcher can be getting on with, assuming that either he/she is not directly involved with interviewing or it is a postal questionnaire. As the early interviews are completed or questionnaires returned, initial coding work for computer analysis can be started. Where interviewers are employed, checks should be made on their progress to ensure that all questions are being asked in the way that was intended and their completion of the forms is up to standard. If interviewers are being paid by completion rate this aspect is of particular importance, as their interest in the project is likely to be much less than their interest in being paid! On this latter point, prompt payment can go far in maintaining the quality of an interviewer's work. Further information on the mechanics of data collection is investigated in Chapter 6.

## Stage 8  Data coding and analysis

In the preparatory stages of the project the type of analysis should have been specified in general terms and reinforced following the pilot stage. If computers are to be used, which invariably they will for all or part of the analysis, then the requirements of the software package will have been taken into account in the questionnaire design. Therefore coding the questionnaires into a form that the computer can read will be undertaken before statistical analysis takes place. Some questionnaires can be scanned and the information coded immediately. In other surveys, questionnaires are stored on portable computers which are used in the interview thereby allowing the coding of information quickly. With telephone surveys the interviewer will often be seated by a computer to record and code the information directly. However, there still remain interviewers with clip boards and paper questionnaires, or surveys where post-interview analysis for coding purposes remains a distinct stage before the statistical analysis can begin.

When it comes to the analysis, computers clearly offer much greater speed and sophistication than manual calculations – providing the sample is relatively large. For smaller surveys where the sample size is perhaps less than 100 respondents and the purpose is largely descriptive, the researcher should question whether computer analysis really will save time. This aspect, though, should have been established earlier in the planning process, rather than having collected the data the researcher now wondering how to analyse it.

Having loaded the appropriate information onto the computer, the analysis of the data is performed and results appear for the first time. This can be one of the most exciting stages in the research process. Whilst you may have a feel for the data, having undertaken some interviews or supervised the coding, the first appearances of frequency tables on the computer screen can be quite gripping. The data have truly become information. Inevitably some results will not have been anticipated and are surprising or give a different slant to what was expected, and this adds to the exhilaration. Following this initial stage, the data must be analysed and statistical tests performed in a systematic way. This is more fully explained in Chapter 7.

## Stage 9  Report and presentation preparation

The final stage for the researcher is often the writing of a report of the research findings. Additionally this may involve giving a presentation where the key points are put across. What then happens may be beyond the control of the researcher, but many reports will include suggestions for further work or recommendations for a suitable course of action. These aspects emphasize the importance of a clear brief and objectives that are understood by all concerned. In the area of academic research the findings may be reported in a journal article or written up in a thesis and are therefore publicly available. However, in consultancy, reports may be confidential and written solely for the company which has commissioned the research. The techniques of report writing and presentation are developed in Chapter 8.

## 3.4 Writing tenders for consultancy projects

Commissioning consultants to undertake research is common practice both within and outside the tourism industry (Brunt, 1995). Tender documents for consultancy projects involve the researcher/consultant outlining how they would plan to do the project and what they will charge if they are awarded the contract. It can be seen, therefore, that for this type of research project consultants need to be able to demonstrate the ability to plan projects clearly before any data collection takes place in anticipation of what the client will require. This is normally done in the form of a written statement called a tender document or proposal. Consultants tender for all kinds of research work and as such the nature of tender proposals varies accordingly. In the context of this book, where some kind of survey research may be specified, a typical proposal would normally have to demonstrate:

- an understanding of the problem;
- an explanation of the methods to be used in collecting the data;
- an explanation of how the data will be analysed;
- details of who will be carrying out the work and what are their credentials;
- the number of client meetings and nature of interim reports;
- the presentation of results – presentation, report, or perhaps a management plan;
- a clear schedule of the programme of work for the project;
- that the consultant has all the necessary facilities to run the project (e.g. computing facilities);
- if a subcontractor is to be used, what credentials and experience are available (the proposal must provide information about the subcontractor on other aspects in as much depth as you would expect from a proposal to be completed solely in house);
- that the consultant's resources are not over committed;
- the costs to be paid by the client;
- the fees to be paid to the consultant.

On these last aspects, those of cost/fees for the project, it is often the case that the available budget is only known to the client or contracting agency. Some contracting agencies will stipulate a maximum budget in the invitation to tender whilst others may be unsure of what their project should cost; some may specifically decide not to indicate any financial information at all. The decision to do this to a certain extent depends on the nature of the project and experience of the contracting agency. If a budget is indicated in the tender then it is unlikely that consultants will strive to offer a lower amount (assuming the budget indicated is acceptable). However, if the contracting agency does not outline what the maximum budget is, consultants may state a low fee in the hope of receiving further work from the client or a high fee as an 'off-chance'. In the opinion of the author, it is preferable for clients to indicate clearly what the maximum budget for a given project is. Then consultants decide whether or not they are interested in the project and can detail what they will provide for the given price. As such the client will receive proposals that are better considered as the consultant must win the contract on the strength of their proposals, methods of data collection and analysis rather than the price.

## Summary

According to Moser (1958) planning a survey involves 'a combination of technical and organizational decisions.' Often this involves much 'to-ing and fro-ing' between considerations of what is appropriate in a technical sense and the constraints posed by the demands of time and money whilst not losing sight of the project aims and objectives. Inevitably research projects differ and the emphasis of different stages in the research process will similarly vary. For example, a project which essentially comes from an academic background may have a much greater focus on a review of literature than would be the case for a consultancy project.

Of crucial importance is the identification of what information is required and how this will be collected. Reviewing literature and secondary sources fully can save considerable time and expense. Of equal importance in the planning process is the pilot stage. This is often neglected or considered a nuisance but can reveal important results which will help shape the overall design of the project.

## Exercises

1  Having read this chapter, discuss the appropriateness of the method of planning a research project outlined in relation to four different types of survey methodology.
2  Explain why the time spent reviewing literature and searching for secondary data sources is worthwhile.
3  Why is it necessary to consider data analysis requirements prior to data collection?

## Further reading

Veal, A.J. (1992). *Research methods for leisure and tourism: A practical guide*. London: Longman/ ILAM.

The third chapter of Veal's book is dedicated to planning a research project in this field. The explanation covers the whole of the research project and includes reference to the tendering process for consultancy type projects.

Hedrick, T.E., Bickman, L. and Rog, D.J. (1993). *Applied research design: A practical guide*. London: Sage Publications.

This book focusses on overcoming some of the main stumbling blocks when designing research projects. It shows how to refine research questions, monitor projects, assess human and physical resources, manage the data collection, analysis and interpretation.

# 4     *Selecting a sample*

## Learning objectives

- Understand the need for sampling.
- Understand how to determine a sampling unit and construct an appropriate sampling frame.
- Be aware of the range of different types of sampling and know where it is appropriate to use them.
- Appreciate the necessary criteria when deciding the size of the sample.

## 4.1 Overview

Market research in travel and tourism is undertaken by organizations to answer research questions. These answers may be used to inform management decisions. For instance, a tour operator may want to know what trust people have in their brochures, or what types of recreational activities their customers are looking for while on a short break to a luxury hotel in the countryside. Moreover, market research may be undertaken to establish the potential for a new type of holiday product in guided tours of antique markets and auctions. The results of surveys in such areas often include general statements about respondents' feelings and opinions. However, in finding answers to these sorts of questions the researcher is faced not only with the difficulty of selecting suitable methods of data collection and survey design, but also to decide whom to ask. With market research which focusses on attitudes to existing products, the current customers could be asked to comment, unless there are proposals which will dramatically change the customer profile. However, with market research which is associated with establishing new products, whom should the researcher ask?

In addition to whom to ask, how many people's views are needed? Often it is not feasible to ask everybody who has purchased a holiday, but asking too few people may not provide a sufficient amount of reliable data on which to base a management decision. The aim of this chapter is to address these issues in a practical and pragmatic way.

## 4.2 What is sampling?

In market research investigations it is rare that every conceivable person associated with a product or topic will be included in the investigation where quantitative analysis is likely to be a feature. Commonly a small portion is selected for data collection and analysis, and on which conclusions are drawn and management decisions taken. This is the process known as sampling. A sample can be thought of as a 'mini-picture' of the whole group from which it is drawn. This group is termed the 'population'. In this context the population may well be all those who have bought a particular product, or perhaps all those who might be expected to buy the product. Whilst the population in this case relates to a group of people, in other types of social research this is not necessarily the case. Research can be carried out on 'populations' of beaches and factories as well as the opinions or behaviour of people.

It is important at this point to remember the distinctions between quantitative and qualitative approaches to data collection and the purpose of the market research itself. If, for example, the aim of the research is to gain the opinions of the National Park Officers of England and Wales, given that there are only ten in total, it would be appropriate to contact all ten. Here, qualitative in-depth interviews may be a suitable method of data collection rather than a structured questionnaire where the small number allows for little in the way of statistical analysis. If, however, a company has sold 250 000 holidays to customers in a season, the opportunity for in-depth interviews with all of them is clearly inappropriate, unnecessary and probably not achievable. In this case quantitative analysis drawn from a sample of this population of tourists is much more appropriate. This is not to suggest that qualitative methods  are not possible nor undesirable on such a large population, but more that such conditions allow for the opportunity of statistical testing. Whilst sampling can be applicable to both quantitative and qualitative approaches, the focus here will be to give greater attention to market research of a quantitative nature.

In these circumstances, using a sample can provide several advantages:

1 Samples are more cost effective against the time it would take to contact the whole population and the cost this would involve.
2 Because samples are based on an 'achievable' number of responses, the focus can move more to the quality of the information provided rather than the quantity.
3 Sampling can allow conclusions to be made of the larger population.

However, if these advantages are to be achieved there are several important considerations to be made:

1 How will the sample be selected from the population?
2 How large should the sample be?
3 To what extent can the sample be considered reliable?

There are undoubtedly examples of studies where insufficient attention is given to these considerations and worthless information was produced from 'biased samples' (that is those samples which differ in a fundamental way from the population from which they are drawn). However, it should be remembered that although sampling is often referred to as a problematical area in research it is not the only area where bias or errors can occur. In preceding chapters errors in the selection of methods of data collection and poor planning have been shown to produce poor results. In the following chapters it will be shown that weaknesses in questionnaire and data analysis can also result in useless information being produced.

There are some good examples of dramatically biased samples. Perhaps the best known of  is the public opinion poll of the 1936 presidential election in the United States (Young, 1966; Moser and Kalton, 1993; and Nachmias and Nachmias,1981). Here an incorrect result was predicted because of a major error in the sampling frame. Ten million people were identified from sources such as telephone directories. In 1936 few poorer people had telephones and hence these voters were excluded from the survey. On the election day, while the prediction had suggested a victory for Landon, the poorer individual voted for Roosevelt. Hence the sample was not representative of the voting population. Errors in sampling methods may have also been behind incorrect opinion polls in the lead up to the 1992 general election in the United Kingdom. Here the opinion polls had predicted a victory for the Labour Party some weeks before the election, and days before the election the vast majority predicted a hung parliament. So following the Conservative election victory attention turned to the obvious mistakes made. *The Economist* (1992) suggested three reasons for the failure to accurately predict the result:

1 Opinion polls measure the 'mood of the moment'. On the day many 'don't knows' became Conservative voters because of effective last minute campaigning.
2 People lied. Voters may have wanted to give the current Conservative government a scare when responding to an interviewer, but in the privacy of the polling booth remained loyal.
3 Sampling error. Because of tight newspaper deadlines, interviewing (often of approximately 1000–1400 people) had to be completed by 4 pm. Thus, on weekdays interviewers in the morning and mid-afternoon tended to pick up a higher proportion of people out of work who were more likely to vote Labour.

In analysing these reasons it is true that a time component is applicable to any survey and external factors may change the result. For example a holiday company may have strongly favourable results for a new product but a change in exchange rates, terrorism, pollution or some other external factor not easily predicted could reverse this. The fact that people may have lied is something which is perhaps a researcher's worst nightmare. However, as previously mentioned, a range of different methods of data collection and careful questioning can reduce this problem. For opinion pollsters to be guilty of sampling error would appear surprising given the reputations of the organizations involved. What this example stresses is the need to select a representative sample from a population of appropriate size which is not biased. How this ideal can be achieved will now be considered.

## 4.3  Selecting a sample

### Sampling unit

When contemplating undertaking a sample survey it is important to define what is termed the sampling unit. This relates to a single member of the survey population. Within the field of market research this is commonly an individual who possesses certain characteristics which are important to the objectives of the survey. For example in the P&O case study described in Chapter 2 the sampling unit was defined as people of a particular age, socio-economic group who accepted the idea of cruising and had the ability to pay for this type of product. However, as mentioned in the previous section, a sampling unit may not always be a person. Sampling units can be drawn from destinations, types of holiday and so on.

### Types of population

The population from which a sample is drawn can have one of two important characteristics: they may be finite or infinite. A finite population is one where the whole population is known and can be counted. For example, the population of tourists undertaking a particular type of holiday with a company is likely to be known as their names and addresses will have been stored by the company on a database and can be easily accessed. Alternatively there may be situations where the population is not easily defined, hence the term infinite population. An example of this can occur at tourist attractions where no charge is made for entry. The staff of the site may be unaware of exactly how many visitors they receive each year. Moreover there may be little or no information about the characteristics of visitors or visits (finding this out may be the objectives of the survey). Under these conditions deciding who and how to sample is clearly more problematical. There may also be situations faced by market researchers between these two extremes. For instance the total number of visitors to a site may be known, but little about when visits take place or the socio-demographic make up of the visitors. To deal with this situation is no easy matter and what is presented in the following sections represents a pragmatic solution to try and compensate for the inherent bias which may occur when selecting a sample of individuals for inclusion in the survey.

## Sampling frame

A sampling frame is a list of the sampling units together with other information which enables a fair sample to be drawn. The main requirement here is that each of the sampling units must have an equal chance of being part of the survey. This is achievable in the situation where the names and addresses of all customers are known, in that the total number is known and checks can be made to ensure that no name is duplicated or omitted. However, as mentioned in the previous section, there are often situations where it is not possible to construct a truly complete sampling frame. It is worth considering why this may be the case before some solutions as to how to cope with the problem are put forward.

## Errors in sampling frames

The following are some of the main errors which are commonly found with sampling frames. The details presented below have been developed from the work of Moser and Kalton (1993) and Frankfort-Nachmias and Nachmias (1992):

### 1 The information is incorrect

This can occur because mistakes were made in entering names and addresses when the list was written. Often lists of names and addresses are compiled for purposes other than the needs of a future survey. Moreover, such lists quickly become out of date, with people moving away.

### 2 The information is incomplete

This commonly occurs because the need for a sampling frame was never envisaged. Many tourist attractions are unlikely to know who visits their site. Similarly transport carriers may have some information where travel tickets are posted to an address or via an agent but not about travellers who purchase at a rail or coach station.

### 3 The information is duplicated

This occurs when lists are combined to develop a sampling frame. For example, a tour operator may wish to send postal questionnaires to a sample of customers who have purchased a holiday from the company in the last five years. Although the names and addresses are known for all the customers, some will have purchased a holiday more than once and therefore may appear on the same sample frame several times. As such, the sample drawn from this list may be biased as some holidaymakers will have a greater chance of being included in the sample. If you assume that frequent purchasers are more favourable towards the company, then such a biased sample may ultimately produce results that are not truly representative. In this example this is on top of the potential problem that going back five years will undoubtedly produce names and addresses that no longer exist, so the sample may be biased in terms of a higher response rate from those who used the company more recently and have not moved house.

## 4 The information is clustered

The problem here is that perhaps several people live at a single address but the purpose of the survey is to interview a particular member of that household. Thus the precise definition of sampling units (particular individuals in this case) is not possible from the sampling frame available. Another instance where this type of problem can occur is at tourist attractions where it is known that a certain proportion of visitors come from within a five-mile radius, ten-mile radius or from particular towns and cities. As the survey focusses on individual visitors this information is helpful in gaining an opinion about the proportions who should be interviewed from these locations but not about who the visitors are or their characteristics.

## 5 The information includes aspects not applicable

Another similar problem is that names and addresses may well exist but only certain types of individual are required for the survey. The survey may need to contact individuals of a particular gender, age or some other aspect such as those holidaymakers who went on a particular excursion as part of their holiday. Hence the list includes information which is not applicable but may not include the extra information needed to identify the particular sampling units (in this case certain holidaymakers) which are required for the survey.

**Methods of coping where sampling frames are incomplete**

Thus there may be many instances where the market researcher in travel and tourism is faced with the problem that developing a sampling frame, and hence selecting a true and reliable sample from it, is fraught with difficulties. It is easy at this point to fall into the trap of assuming that it is possible to compensate for all the potential errors in a sampling frame by simply increasing the sample size. Whilst it is true that, other things being equal, a larger sample stands a better chance of being more representative of the population than a smaller sample, a sample that is fundamentally flawed remains biased.

Where sampling frames are not available, complete or are otherwise suspect, additional aspects of the population can be considered to develop a procedure to assist in the better selection of a sample. These steps can be considered before and after the data collection.

To illustrate the types of problem, consider the situation faced by the researcher when undertaking a site visitor survey at a tourist attraction. We can assume that the site manager is unaware who the visitors are (in terms of age, gender, type of group, etc.), where they have come from, or their attitudes towards certain aspects of the site. In the main, answers to these areas are the objectives of the survey. The method of data collection for at least a part of the survey has been decided as a face-to-face interview with users of the site. This type of scenario is quite common in this area and the development of a suitable sampling frame requires careful consideration. The following steps represent a pragmatic way of approaching this type of problem:

*1 Who to ask?*

Perhaps the first step is to determine who to ask. In the situation outlined above, any person visiting the tourist attraction for recreational purposes is eligible to be included in the survey. One aspect which should be considered is at what age visitors become suitable. Clearly the responses, attitudes, decision-making and purchasing requirements of young children may well be different to those of adults. Extreme care should be taken when contemplating interviews with children, and only ever with the full cooperation of parents (see ethical considerations in Chapter 1). It may be preferable in situations where the opinions of children are important to design a separate survey (possibly with some comparable questions to a survey of adults). In this sense it could be much easier to train interviewers in the particular requirements of the survey, gain permission and inform the local police of the aims and methods of the survey.

Although site surveys at tourist attractions with face-to-face interviews can achieve a high response rate, some people will refuse to cooperate. In the literature those taking part in a survey are called 'respondents' and hence a response rate of 90 per cent would indicate that 90 per cent of those approached for interview agreed to and satisfactorily completed the interview. Thus, in order to be able to report the response rate, it is important to keep a record of non-respondents. If the response rate is very low then a judgement may have to be made as to the reliability of the results.

## 2 When should data be collected?

In deciding on what days to interview, consideration should be given to the patterns of visits at the tourist attraction over the season. For example, the number of visits made to the attraction is likely to be different at the beginning and end of the season than in the middle or following a significant advertising campaign. Moreover, there may be particular days when the usage of the site is untypical when compared to the rest of the year. Special events and visits by celebrities or public holidays could easily distort a sample drawn where the number of days allocated for interviewing included a high proportion of days when the site was unusually overcrowded. In addition, variations in site usage can occur on a daily and weekly basis. At informal recreation sites such as country parks, dog walkers may visit the site on a very regular basis, perhaps early in the morning. Later in the day, the site might attract groups of people who visit the site less frequently than the dog walkers but make more use of the facilities provided. Furthermore, on weekdays there may be a higher proportion of retired people compared to weekend days when more families are likely to visit. At many tourist attractions there will be differences between the number and type of people within and outside the main school holiday periods over and above seasonal variations.

In deciding when to interview, an awareness of the sorts of variations on different types of day is important. Ideally the number of days selected should reflect these variations. The number of days needed will be related to the sample size, length of interview, number of interviewers and characteristics of the site. Interviewing should take place on at least three days of a similar type.

### 3 When to interview in relation to the visit

For the majority of surveys the end of the visit is normally the best time to approach people for an interview. In this sense visitors to the tourist attraction will have had chance to make use of all of the site facilities they are going to. If interviewing takes place during the visit respondents may not be able to answer all the questions because they may not have had the opportunity of gaining an opinion about facilities they have yet to make use of.

An exception to this was undertaken by Brunt (1990). Site surveys were used as one of several methods in establishing why visitors had selected certain tourist attractions for their day trips. In this particular instance it was found, after the pilot stage, that interviewing people as they arrived at the site provided the best results. This was because some respondents found that the experience of the visit (whether positive or negative) caused difficulty in remembering why they had decided to visit the site in the first place. A typical response to an open question of 'why did you decide to visit this site today' was 'I am not sure, but we are certainly not coming back'. Hence interviewing people at the end of their visit proved unsatisfactory. However, most site surveys at tourist attractions require respondents to indicate what they feel about specific aspects of the site they have just visited. Thus the most practical time to interview is at the end of their visit.

### 4 Where on the site to interview

Given that it is advisable to interview at the end of the visit, it is necessary to find a suitable point near to the site exit. Ideally, if there is a location where all visitors pass on their way out of the site, then all would have an equal chance of being included in the survey. As equal chance is a crucial aim in developing a fair sample, effort should be made in establishing a suitable interview point.

There may be some sites, such as those in open countryside, where there is no single exit. Here, careful and systematic observations can be used to determine the main 'natural' exit points. Then, either an interviewer can be placed at each exit, or a single interviewer could visit each in rotation.

## 5 *Whom to approach*

As every person visiting the tourist attraction on a survey day has been deemed to be eligible for interview, then each should, as far as possible, have the same chance of being part of the survey. In the example which has been developed here, the population of the visitors to the site is not known, and interviewing say every tenth person to exit may leave interviewers with little to do during parts of the day. However, instructing interviewers to decide for themselves whom to approach is likely to introduce bias. This is because some interviewers will naturally select certain types of people who they feel are more approachable and likely to agree to an interview. In a similar sense, individuals who present themselves for interview should not be permitted to be included. This is because self-selection may introduce bias in the form of producing results with a disproportionately high number of respondents who had 'something to say'.

The Tourism and Recreation Research Unit (1983) recommend that the 'next-to-pass' technique be adopted in these circumstances. In short, the interviewer is suitably located and the first person to pass this point is approached for interview. When this interview is completed (if agreement to take part is reached) the next person to pass is similarly approached. Obviously, if somebody passes whilst an interview is in progress then they are not chased after or required to wait! With a fair number of survey days, interview points and well trained interviewers then this technique should yield satisfactory results. The interviewer has no control over when a visitor decides to leave the site and pass the interview point and hence this removes interviewer bias in the selection of respondents.

## 6 *What about groups?*

Inevitably at tourist attractions people are highly likely to visit in groups, either as a family, group of friends or some other combination. It is preferable if the interview is undertaken by a single respondent. Often this occurs naturally if the interviewer truly selects the first person in the group to pass and addresses the questions directly to this individual. However, occasionally there can be a problem with respondents conferring with other members of the group or even disagreements being caused by the questions. Trained interviewers may have to be permitted to exercise a certain amount of practical judgement in such situations.

## 7  Weighting

Observations made at the site to help develop a sampling frame and define the sampling unit will have established times of the day when the site has most of its visitors. Unfortunately it may not be possible to increase the number of interviewers to account for this. Thus by using the next-to-pass technique there may be certain times when many more people are passing the interview point and leaving the site because the interviewer is occupied. For example, it could be found that half of those interviewed on a particular day had travelled to the site by coach but observations had shown that a higher proportion of visitors had arrived by car. Some account should be made of this to allow for possible errors in the results. Thus some replies in the analysis stage could be adjusted or 'weighted' to allow for the higher numbers of coach trippers interviewed than were actually present on the site.

### Summary: selecting a sample

When selecting a sample for the situation outlined in the preceding section, it has been shown that the construction of a sampling frame depends upon factors which include:

- awareness of the population;
- definition of the sampling unit;
- patterns of site use;
- type of survey method.

In many instances in travel and tourism, developing a sampling frame can be difficult to achieve. Awareness of the possible limitations is important and must be fairly reported. Whilst all surveys aim to provide the best possible sampling frame from which to select a sample, the purpose and requirements of the survey should be borne in mind. Clearly the accuracy required from a survey, where the results will prompt important decisions, is higher than in an exploratory, descriptive study. If there is a mismatch between the level of precision and accuracy required of the results and the ability to construct a suitable sampling frame then the only recourse is to extend the range of methods of data collection. Moreover, any limitations known in relation to the sampling frame must be fairly discussed in the report so that subsequent management decisions are appropriately informed.

# 4.4 Types of sampling

Previous sections have stressed the importance of every eligible member of a survey population having an equal chance of selection in a sample. This is an important principle within sampling and as far as possible the market researcher must try to ensure that this is the case if the results are to be viable. At a general level there are two basic types of sampling which follow this condition, which can then be subdivided into a number of particular types. The two basic types of sampling where the 'equal chance' principle applies are probability sampling and random sampling. Before defining these it should be remembered that often the types of sampling procedures used are not mutually exclusive, but overlap with each other to a certain extent. For a specific research project it is common to find several sampling techniques being adopted.

## Probability sampling

In situations where the extent of the survey population is known, an individual sampling unit (often in tourism an individual person) has a known chance of being included in the survey. For example, if a company in the tourism industry has developed an accurate sampling frame of its customer base, then the potential population is known. If this is, say, 200 000 individual customers and a sample size of 2000, then each customer must have a 1 in 100 chance of being included in the sample. The calculation of the probability in this instance is behind the concept of probability sampling. However, of equal importance is that the actual selection of the 2000 individual respondents must be done on a random basis. Methods of selecting a sample randomly will be discussed shortly; first it is necessary to define what we mean by random sampling.

## Random sampling

Random sampling is almost the same as probability sampling with one slight exception, which is pertinent to the topic of this book. As has been shown, there may be situations where the population in a survey is not known. With the case of informal recreation sites, which are admission free, this is often the case and the total number of visitors from year to year is estimated rather than being calculated. Hence true probability sampling is not possible. The principle of random selection can still apply, but the probability of inclusion in a survey cannot, as the population size is unknown. Take for example interviewing on a next-to-pass basis 200 people leaving a beach. They are selected on a random basis but it is not known whether the 200 interviewed are from a population of 1000, 1500 or 5000 beach-goers on that day or over a season. Awareness of the limitations this may cause in terms of the inability to predict from these 200 the attitudes of all visitors to the beach is clear. However, this should not suggest that such a survey would be worthless, as descriptive studies or 'straw polls' can be of much value in certain situations where predictions and generalizations of the rest of the population are not necessary.

Nevertheless, probability sampling, where a population is known, can be seen as preferable wherever it is possible. This is because statistical techniques can be used to suggest the amount of 'error' between the sample and its representativeness with the rest of the population. This specific aspect will be investigated in a later section.

Returning to the different types of sampling, it can be seen that probability sampling and random sampling share many characteristics. Both methods involve the random selection of sampling units in a survey. Because they are so similar in many respects, the specific difference is often ignored and either the term 'probability sampling' is loosely used to include 'random sampling' or vice versa. Having defined the starting point, it is now possible to look in more detail at some more specific types of sampling methods which are based on the principles of equal chance and random selection.

## 1  Simple and systematic random sampling

Simple random sampling is a method which is similar to a lottery. In the case of a known list of customers of say 100 000 names, a sample of 1000 could be drawn by placing all the names on paper, placing them in a very large hat and drawing 1000 from it. Such a method in practice would be somewhat cumbersome and computers are able to generate random numbers to achieve the same goal. In a survey it would be necessary to draw 1000 different names, thus once a name had been selected it would not be eligible for selection again. In theoretical terms statisticians would start to complain about this as the second name drawn from that hat would have a 1 in 99 999 chance of being drawn unless the first name was replaced in the hat. However, in surveys it is not practical or desirable to interview the same person more than once. Obviously some commonsense and judgement are necessary to be fair yet pragmatic. If random numbers are used then the next random number selected should suffice if duplication occurs.

To overcome some of the potential pitfalls with simple random sampling, the selection of respondents can be carried out in a more systematic way. Taking the same scenario where the population is known, if a sample of 1000 is required from the list of 100 000 names, then every 100th name could be taken. The starting point could be determined randomly and then every 100th name selected from this point.

Simple and systematic samples are used where the members of a population are similar or homogenous. No account is made of any particular characteristic of the population and every member of the population is given an equal chance of inclusion in the survey. As we have already seen, in travel and tourism full knowledge of the population may not be possible or it may not be homogenous. If the latter aspect is the case then the following method of sampling may be more appropriate.

## 2 Stratified random sampling

Where information about the population of a survey is known, it is possible to divide the population into smaller sub-samples or 'strata'. It is common in our field for this to be done on the basis of socio-demographic characteristics such as gender, age, socio-economic group or a categorization of previous purchasing behaviour. A particular sampling unit such as a potential individual respondent can be placed in the sub-sample only once. After each sub-sample has been determined the individual sampling units are randomly selected from each sub-sample.

In effect this process is similar to probability sampling where every member of a population has an equal chance of inclusion in the survey and selection is conducted randomly. Here the population is divided into strata, and within each stratum every member has an equal chance of inclusion and the selection is random.

The main purpose of this method of sampling is to achieve a more reliable sample. However, a great deal of knowledge about the population is required, over and above the extent of the population, if stratification is to be workable. If, for example, within a survey population there are clearly identifiable groups where there is a high level of similarity (homogeneity) within the groups and there are many differences (heterogeneity) between the groups then stratification may be worthwhile. This may particularly be the case if the distinct groups vary in size. For instance, if a company has a small minority who complain about their product then they may not be sufficiently recognized in a large survey. If, however, they are characterized as a group by several easily identifiable factors then the problem could be much greater than is apparent. This could, for example, be a group of holidaymakers who are identified by their age, social class, or those who stayed at a specific resort.

There remains the problem, though, in whether such groups can be identified 'prior' to the main survey to enable this type of sampling method to be performed. Computer analysis of survey results allows for such groups to be selected out from the sample and be analysed specifically and separately from the rest. Thus prior selection and stratification as well as not often being achievable (due to lack of prior knowledge) are not always necessary.

Perhaps the main use of this type of sampling method in the field of travel and tourism is where the residence of individuals is known and can be stratified. To demonstrate this take, for instance, a survey of season ticket holders to and from an island for a ferry operator. Season tickets are purchased by commuters to the island and to the mainland. Prior to the survey the population of all season ticket holders was found to be 20000. Of these 15000 live on the mainland and 5000 live on the island. If it is decided that a sample of 1000 should be interviewed then appropriate proportions could easily be calculated, i.e. 750 mainlanders and 250 islanders.

## Cluster sampling

Where surveys cover very large areas, such as whole countries, the types of sampling methods described to this point may not be very cost effective. Consider, for example, a company wishing to conduct a nationwide survey of a sample of its customers using personal interviews. Random sampling may well yield a list of potential respondents spread widely across the country but thinly in some areas, thus interviewers may have to travel very long distances to conduct a small number of interviews. To overcome this type of problem the researcher identifies groupings or clusters of respondents in a particular area. A range of clusters are selected randomly and then within each cluster, respondents are again selected on a random basis. This method of sampling is called 'cluster sampling' (some older texts may refer to this as area sampling). This method can also be useful where the extent of the survey population is not fully known, as shown in the following example.

*Example: travel agent services*

**BACKGROUND**

*A branch of a travel agency has been established for the first time in a town. A survey is decided to ascertain the awareness of this venture amongst the resident population of the surrounding area, but no complete list of all residents is available.*

**STAGES**

*1 A map is used to define the boundary of potential users of the shop.*
*2 The area within this boundary is divided into segments reflecting all the areas, both residential and non-residential.*
*3 Each segment is numbered.*
*4 A sample of segments is selected on a simple random or systematic basis.*
*5 Within the segments actual residences are numbered.*
*6 Systematic or simple random samples of residences are selected.*
*7 Individuals within the selected residences are contacted for interview.*

In this example, two clusters are used; segments within the defined boundary and residences within each segment. In some surveys it may be necessary for several stages of clustering to take place in this way. Where this occurs, the process is sometimes referred to as multi-stage sampling.

A variation on this theme can be found with what is termed 'multi-phase sampling'. The difference between 'multi-stage' and 'multi-phase' often relates to the latter using a follow-up survey. In the example above a first 'phase' might be to investigate the awareness of the new travel agency outlet. From the results of this, a second 'phase' could be to develop a follow-up survey amongst those respondents who answered a particular question in a specific way. For example, further details could be sought from those who have indicated that they are planning to book a holiday in the next six months, or those who have asked to be informed of special offers. Thus multi-phase sampling could be used to first gain a general picture and follow up with more detailed (and longer) interviews in a subsequent phase with particular sub-sets of respondents. In all phases the respondents are always selected randomly.

## Summary: probability sampling methods

Simple random, systematic random, stratified random, cluster sampling and its variants are the main methods of probability sampling. All methods are similar in that the probability of a sampling unit within a survey population being included in the sample is known and the selection of sampling units is conducted randomly. It is now worth considering, briefly, what the opposite of this is.

### Non-probability/non-random sampling

In situations where the population is not known or there is insufficient time to build a sampling frame, some researchers may turn to non-probability sampling methods. The most commonly used (and criticized) method is called 'quota sampling'. For example, in street surveys interviewers may be required to question certain types of people and are given a 'quota' to complete of each type. The population may be divided in terms of apparent age, social class or other controlling variables upon which the interviewers must make a subjective judgement in the selection of potential respondents. In the opinion of this author, this leaves too much discretion to the interviewer, enabling a significant amount of bias to enter the sample.

## 4.5 Sample size

Moser (1958) stated that 'anyone who ever has to advise on sample designs will know that almost invariably the first question he is asked is – how big a sample do I need?' Many years later, this statement remains true. However, often the question being asked could be more accurately re-phrased to 'what is the minimum number I can get away with?' Selecting the size of the sample is clearly an important question in the design of any survey. All surveys where a sample of the population is used will involve a level of 'sampling error'. This is the difference between what has been found in the results based on the sample and the actual values that would have been found out if everybody in the population had been included in the survey.

It is tempting to assume that by simply enlarging the sample size, problems of error will disappear. However, any sample which is biased in its sampling methods or selection of respondents will remain biased whatever its size. Furthermore, until the sample size becomes a high proportion of the population (say over 20 per cent) then the actual size of the sample is more important than the sample's proportion to the population. Clearly though, an increase in sample size in a survey where the sample is drawn by fair means will reduce the level of sampling error. Thus the sample size often represents a compromise between what is achievable in a pragmatic sense and what is desirable statistically in relation to the concept of sampling error. These two sides of determining sample size will now be evaluated in turn.

## 1 Pragmatic determination of sample size

At several points in this book we have returned to the question 'what is the purpose of the survey' and in deciding on sample size this should again be borne in mind. Where a high level of accuracy is required from the results and forecasting or other generalizations are required from the sample about the rest of the population, then the size of the sample becomes crucial. However, in more descriptive studies, if 350 people out of 500 interviewed requested extra refreshment facilities at a tourist attraction, then a management decision might reasonably be based on this alone. Thus the need for complicated, predictive statistics requiring large samples may be unnecessary. Perhaps the first question to ask is the level of accuracy required from the results in relation to the survey objectives.

At a second level, the researcher should consider what statistical tests will be performed on the data. Here again, there is a relationship with the objectives of the survey. In Chapter 7 we will look at analysing results from surveys and this will show that some statistical tests require a minimum number of responses on which the test can be satisfactorily executed. If an objective of the survey is to investigate how age affects the reaction to a product, then the results might be tabulated as in Table 4.1.

**Table 4.1** *Cross-tabulation of age and opinion of product*

| Age | Opinion of product (1 = excellent, 5 = very poor) | | | | |
|---|---|---|---|---|---|
| | *1* | *2* | *3* | *4* | *5* |
| 16–30 | | | | | |
| 31–45 | | | | | |
| 46–60 | | | | | |
| 61 and over | | | | | |

In Table 4.1 there are 20 cells (5 columns of opinion scores multiplied by 4 rows relating to age category). For a possible relationship between age and opinion to be tested then the sample size needs to be sufficiently large for there to be responses in each cell. The pilot stage in a survey is useful in showing whether the classification of categories is appropriate.

A third level of questioning which helps to determine sample size is the amount of resources the researcher has available. There will be a finite budget in terms of the time available and the costs of the project. The larger the sample the greater the resources required. Larger sizes may therefore result in the need for more staff and an increased number of survey days for interviews. Hence sample size is often influenced by the constraint of the resources available.

At a fourth, and final level, the researcher must consider the anticipated response rate shown by the pilot stage. This is particularly applicable to postal surveys. If the requirements of the survey in terms of the accuracy and statistical analysis call for 1000 completed questionnaires and a response rate of 50 per cent is anticipated, then clearly 2000 questionnaires should be distributed.

To summarize, to determine sample size in a pragmatic way, the researcher should consider:

1 the accuracy required from the results in relation to the objectives of the survey;
2 the requirements of statistical tests in the analysis stage;
3 the available resources of the project;
4 the anticipated response rate.

## 2 Sample size and the calculation of sampling error

Where samples are selected on a random basis the range of sampling error can be calculated according to the laws of probability and statistical theory. For a full discussion of the formulae to perform this calculation, the reader is referred to Moser and Kalton (1993). The formula produces margins of error in percentages in relation to the proportions of respondents answering in a particular way for a given sample size, as indicated in Table 4.2.

**Table 4.2** *Sampling errors in percentages*

| Percentage found in sample | Sample size 30 | 50 | 100 | 500 | 1000 | 3000 |
|---|---|---|---|---|---|---|
| 50 | 19.6 | 14.9 | 10.3 | 4.5 | 3.2 | 1.8 |
| 40 or 60 | ★ | 14.6 | 10.1 | 4.4 | 3.1 | 1.8 |
| 30 or 70 | ★ | ★ | 9.5 | 4.1 | 2.9 | 1.7 |
| 20 or 80 | ★ | ★ | ★ | 3.6 | 2.5 | 1.5 |
| 10 or 90 | ★ | ★ | ★ | 2.6 | 1.9 | 1.1 |

★ Shows that the sampling error percentage is greater than the original size

NB The percentages in this table are calculated to the 95 per cent level. This means that there is a 95 per cent probability that the percentages found in a survey lie within a range equal to the percentage found plus or minus the percentage shown in the table. The table shows the range of sampling error for the results of simple random surveys with samples of varying sizes.

To understand the table, consider that in a survey of visitors to a tourist attraction 50 per cent were found to be local residents and 50 per cent were tourists. If the sample of a known population was 30 people, the actual amount for the whole population could be expected to be between 30 and 70 per cent of this result (that is plus or minus 19.6 per cent of the result found in the survey). If the sample size is increased to 3000 people, the actual value for the whole population (for a similar 50 per cent result) could be expected to be between 48 and 53 per cent (plus or minus 1.8 per cent of the result found in the survey). As the proportions of people answering a question in a particular way change then so does the sampling error. For example if it was found in a survey of 3000 that 90 per cent were in favour of providing an additional facility and 10 per cent were against it, then the real value for the survey population could be expected to be plus or minus 1.1 per cent of this figure.

A problem arises on which question in a survey to focus the sampling error to inform the sample size. Clearly a practical solution is to set the standard of accuracy on the most crucial question or issue in the survey. If, for example, the main objective of the survey is to test the different reactions to the tourist attraction by residence of the respondent, then this is the best question to set sample size against. If a survey has several objectives of equal importance, then the subject where there is most disagreement or variation should be taken as the basis to inform sample size.

This method assumes some knowledge of the population and furthermore stresses the need for carefully conducted pilot surveys. What has not been mentioned in this context, is the influence of response rates on these calculations. Clearly the accuracy of sampling error calculations becomes increasingly suspect if non-response rates are very high.

## Summary

In the field of market research in travel and tourism, where we are often concerned with the attitudes of customers to the quality of products, sample surveys are vital and hence it is important to understand the nature of sampling. This chapter has introduced some of the basic concepts of sampling theory applicable to the readership of this book. The reasons why a sample survey is chosen are often due to considerations of cost and access to respondents. In many instances it may not be possible to define a population and construct a sampling frame and the chapter has demonstrated compensatory strategies where this occurs.

The selection of sampling units needs to be random and fair if the results are to be assumed to be unbiased and precise. This aspect is at the heart of sampling theory. However, practical techniques such as those involved with stratification provide the researcher with an opportunity to select a sample which will give maximum utility and cost effectiveness to the research project.

# Exercises

1 Outline the salient factors to ensure that a sample is representative in the following types of survey:

(a) household survey;
(b) site survey;
(c) postal survey.

2 Justify the main criteria for determining sample size.

# Further reading

Barnet, V. (1991). *Sample survey: Principles and methods*. London: Edward Arnold.

This book is written for students and professionals and assesses the many facets of sample surveys. Particular emphasis is given to the role of sampling when deciding on the approach for data collection, detailed explanation of sampling methods and how to overcome some of the technical difficulties when conducting a sample survey.

Moser, Sir C.A. and Kalton, G. (1993). *Survey methods in social investigation*. Second edition. London: Heinemann.

This book has been recommended for other topics and in this context has four chapters devoted to sampling. These guide the reader from initial ideas and basics of sampling through the different types of sample design and have useful sections on sample size, sampling frames and response errors.

*Designing a questionnaire*

## Learning objectives

- To be able to a design workable questionnaire.
- To understand the differences between the principal types of question.
- To appreciate the potential errors when wording questions.

There is a wide variety of different types of questionnaire used in tourism for both academic research and industry application. Structured questionnaires are those which ask precise, concrete questions prepared in advance to facilitate quantitative analysis. Unstructured questionnaires, sometimes referred to as interview guides, also aim at precision and contain topic areas where respondents are less restricted in their answers. This latter type is common within in-depth interviews and focus groups.

## 5.1 Question types

Broadly speaking all questions are either **open** (free-response) or **closed** (structured).

### Closed questions

A closed question is one in which the respondent is offered a choice of replies. He/she may be asked to tick a box in a self-completion questionnaire, or the answers may be read out to him/her, or shown on a prompt card. Questions of this kind may offer simple alternatives such as yes or no, or a simple list, or something more complex, e.g.:

---

1. Have you visited this site before?
   - ☐ Yes
   - ☐ No

2. How did you travel to this site ?

   - ☐ Car
   - ☐ Walk
   - ☐ Service bus
   - ☐ Bicycle
   - ☐ Coach
   - ☐ Other

3. If it is proven that bracken at recreation sites affects human health, with which of these statements would you agree most ?

   - ☐ A programme of bracken removal/control should be implemented

   - ☐ People should be made aware of the health risks, but the bracken should not be removed

   - ☐ I do not think there is anything to worry about

---

Other types of questions that are essentially closed include ranking and rating scales. Below are some examples:

---

1 Look at the following card and rank the reasons why you decided to visit this attraction.
   (INTERVIEWER TO ASSIST RESPONDENT WITH RANKING AS NECESSARY)
   - ☐ NEARER TO ACCOMMODATION/HOME
   - ☐ CHEAPER THAN OTHER LOCAL ATTRACTIONS
   - ☐ MORE CHOICE OF RIDES
   - ☐ EASY PARKING
   - ☐ LESS WALKING

2 Look at this card and use the scale provided to answer the following question. A score of 5 indicates you believe it to be of great importance and a score of 1 indicates that you believe it to have no importance.

When you decided to stay at this resort how important was the cost?

5    Great importance
4
3
2
1    No importance

3 Indicate which of the following applies to you :
When deciding on a holiday the type of accommodation is the most important consideration.
☐ STRONGLY AGREE
☐ AGREE
☐ UNCERTAIN
☐ DISAGREE
☐ STRONGLY DISAGREE

4 Indicate which of the following applies to you:
How satisfied are you with the helpfulness of staff in this hotel?

☐ VERY SATISFIED
☐ SATISFIED
☐ DISSATISFIED
☐ VERY DISSATISFIED

Reference to the literature will show that there is much debate on the length of the various scoring systems and whether to have an odd or even number of categories. Note here that I have not included a don't know category. In the next section this is discussed more fully.

Thus closed questions can be attitudinal as well as factual. In the last example, if left to their own thoughts, some respondents may have come up with their own proposals. Here the list of alternatives has been derived after careful piloting to ensure that the categories do cover the majority of opinion.

*Advantages of closed questions*

1 Easier and quicker to answer.
2 No writing.
3 Quantification and coding easier.
4 More questions possible in terms of time/ money available.

*Disadvantages of closed questions*

1 Loss of spontaneity and expressiveness (will never know what the respondent would have said if left to their own devices).
2 Bias – in forcing a particular set of answers that might not have occurred to the respondent.
3 Closed questions are often simpler and less subtle as no probing is possible.
4 Loss of rapport with interviewer – some respondents may become irritated because they feel that their real opinions are not represented in the set of alternatives.
5 It is easier for the respondent to cheat.

## Open questions

Open questions are not usually followed by any kind of choice. Answers are recorded in full. In the case of a self-completion questionnaire the amount of space made available will help to determine the length and fullness of the responses obtained. There are several types which are best demonstrated using examples.

1 Open
Why did you decide to go on a day trip today?
RECORD ANSWER

2 Open - with clarification
In the next questions I am going to focus on day trips. This is defined as a journey away from home lasting longer than three hours but not including an overnight stay. Why did you decide to go on a day trip today?

3 Open – with probing
Why did you decide to go on a day trip today?
Followed by probing either from a checklist or left to the interviewer.

*Advantages of open questions*

1 Freedom on the part of the respondent in giving an answer.
2 Spontaneous.

*Disadvantages of open questions*

1 Difficult to code.
2 Hard to analyse quantitatively.
3 Interviewer bias.

Overall there are obviously pros and cons with both types of question type. In order to offset the disadvantages it may be useful to ask the same question topic both ways. With open questions, whilst the answer may be valuable, the interpretation and comparison between respondents may be difficult. With closed questions you cannot be sure that an impromptu sketch contains all the factors that are important.

## Some worked examples illustrating how to decide which type of question system to use

For each of the following scenarios consider whether it is appropriate to use an open or closed type of question system.

1 You want to find out how many people read the *Daily Mirror* yesterday.

   **Answer:** Closed question system. This is a straightforward head count, thus the answer is yes or no. There may be potential problems with the word 'read' being ambiguous.

2 In your survey you aim to ask each head of household what his/her job is.

   **Answer:** If your main 'aim' is to find out precisely what their job is, then an open question system will be required. It is not possible to list all jobs so the question will be open. However, sometimes the interviewer (if present) may need to probe or seek clarification of the response. Answers such as 'engineer' may require the inteviewer to ask for more detail. In other surveys where this is not the main 'aim', often job categories are listed and respondents decide for themselves which is most suited to their situation. In a postal survey, closed questions would have to be used.

3 You want to find out how many people agree with different views about their holiday to the Seychelles, but you do not know what these views are.

**Answer:** To do this properly two surveys are required. To begin with you need to find out what views people have about the Seychelles. Because you do not know what views people have, open questions where interviewers probe for as much information as possible is probably the best method. Then after analysing the results of this survey, closed questions can be constructed. These can then be used to count the number of people who endorse or reject those views about the Seychelles.

4 A product of your company is not selling well to your target market. You only have a few vague suspicions as to why this is so and you want to explore in an empirical way the nature of the problem.

**Answer:** Here your purpose is exploratory. You cannot design closed questions if you only have vague suspicions as to why the product is not selling well. Therefore open questions are required to explore the nature of the problem.

5 You have a list of, say, 30 different characteristics of management in a travel firm. You would like to find out, for each of these characteristics, how many employed persons say it is true of their firm. However you are worried about offering more than 10 characteristics on a show card because you feel they would not properly consider more than that on a single card.

**Answer:** In this case you are trying to find out what opinions people have of the 30 characteristics of management you are studying rather than asking them to describe the characteristics of their firm for themselves. Thus the answer is that a closed question system is needed to count the number of people who say that a given characteristic is true or untrue. The fears about presenting a long list relate to the wording and layout of the questionnaire. These aspects are investigated in the next section.

## 5.2 Wording questions and laying out the questionnaire

The content of the questionnaire is obviously governed by the nature of the survey, but there are many potential problems in the communication of the questions. These types of problem apply to all surveys.

## Language

The language used in the wording of questions is of critical importance. The researcher should give careful thought to how the question will be interpreted by the respondent. There are two salient points to remember when you begin to write your questions:

1 Be clear and concise. Keep questions short, as long sentences which require respondents to concentrate will not be answered accurately.
2 Avoid using jargon. The vocabulary should be simple everyday language (unless to a particular technical audience).

## Familiar words

As a rule, you should always use familiar, simple words. However, occasionally some words are too vague. For example, 'how often', 'how much' and 'how far' may result in answers that are not comparable. Asking 'How much do you drink?' in an open sense is likely to result in a set of replies that either overstate or understate a true reply! In addition, words such as 'good', 'bad', 'regularly', which are not enumerated precisely, do not lend themselves to quantitative analysis.

## Technical terms

Technical words should only be used if the survey is aimed at a specific group of respondents to whom the language is common. Words and phrases such as 'sympathetic planning', 'green tourism', 'sustainable tourism', 'national tourism organization', and 'tour operators' are likely to mean different things to different people. Some may have a genuine and accurate grasp of what is meant by the term, whilst others may respond favourably to stereotyped concepts. The solution here is to ask questions that can be easily understood by all respondents. Technical terms which have to be used may need to be defined or respondents asked to explain what they understand by them.

## Ambiguous questions

Whilst previous sections have suggested that simple, everyday language should be used in the wording of questions, sometimes this can lead to ambiguity. Consider posing the question to different groups of students, 'What kind of course are you on?' This could be answered in terms of degree/HND, sandwich, good, bad, well organized, interesting, difficult, etc. The likelihood is that a range of replies that had no relationship to each other would be produced. If answers cannot be compared, then it becomes impossible to express the data in quantifiable terms. This aspect reinforces the need for all surveys to have a pilot stage to test the usefulness of your questions and thus avoid ambiguity during the main data collection.

## Leading questions

A leading question is one in which the respondent is guided to give a particular answer by the nature of the question. This is clearly unacceptable and leads to the validity of the whole survey being brought into question. For example, 'Most people like to holiday abroad nowadays, would you?' This is a leading question because it is more difficult to answer no than yes. To answer no implies that you are different to 'most' people. These types of questions essentially put words into the mouth of the respondent. It should not be easier to reply 'yes' than to say 'no' or vice versa.

## The don't know problem

This issue is a difficult area, as there will always be some answers which will fall between yes and no, or between agree and disagree. Sometimes questionnaires include a category of 'don't know' or 'no opinion'. However, you should bear in mind that respondents may reply 'don't know' for several reasons. These have been developed from the work of Gardner (1978).

### 1 Interview failure

Perhaps the question was not heard or understood. The interviewer may not have waited long enough for a reply. Maybe the respondent hesitated – 'Well I don't know' ... (down goes the answer) ... 'Yes I suppose I would' – but it is too late, the interviewer is already asking the next question.

## 2  Ignorance

This can occur in two ways. Either the information was not available or the information was available but it was not understood. Preliminary questions will help to sort out those who are not aware of it or who have not had time to consider it. Again the pilot survey would help to sort things out here.

## 3  Indecision

Having considered the matter the respondent can come to no definite view either way. This is a genuine response and you should allow for this. However, it could be argued that a response of 'no opinion' is better than a 'don't know'.

## 4  Indifference

This response relates to respondents who have heard about the issue but do not feel that they need to bother themselves with it. A series of preliminary questions could cover for this, e.g:

(i)    Have you heard about our latest Frequent Traveller Benefits Scheme?
(ii)   Have you had time to consider it?
(iii)  Do you think it matters whether it goes ahead or not?
(iv)   Do you think the scheme should go ahead?

After a negative response to (i) or (ii) there is no need to proceed with the rest.

## Sequence of questions

The sequence of questions is important and is one of the advantages that interviews have over self-completion questionnaires. In interviews the interviewer has control over the sequence of questions whereas with self-completion there is very little control over this aspect. The respondent can look ahead and see what is coming. For both methods there are some general guidelines:

**Introduction** – whether written or spoken, must create interest and motivate the respondent to cooperate. Confidentiality should again be assured. Some of the introduction may come in the form of a covering letter.

**First questions** – these should be interesting, simple and related to the topic you have outlined in your introduction. That way the respondent is assured that he is neither going to be bored nor floored.

**Sequence** – as far as possible the sequence of questions should follow a natural order. To avoid sudden jumps from one topic to another, insert suitable bridging passages.

**'Crux' questions** – should come in the body of the interview, about or just after midway, when rapport is strongest and before boredom or impatience sets in.

**Personal questions** – the general convention is to put these at the end of the questionnaire perhaps with a reminder of confidentiality and an explanation that they are for comparative purposes.

**General to specific** – it should not be possible for answers to be influenced by previous questions. If a respondent is forced to take a stand on one issue, it is much harder for him to modify his position later when other questions suggest different possibilities or require different sorts of comparisons. Once a train of thought has been narrowed to a particular aspect, it becomes difficult to put this in proper perspective when broader issues are involved.

## Checklists and prompt cards

Prompt cards can be used to suggest a wide range of possible answers. They indicate the appropriate frame of reference and help the respondent to think of other possibilities. This may sound like coercion, and indeed an interviewer may unknowingly put stress or a pleasant intonation on some items if he/she has to read out the list. However, prompt cards can be handed to the respondent with a question such as:

---

Please look at this list. Which of the activities mentioned have you undertaken today?

> Nature trail
> Guided walk
> Self-guided walk
> Bird hide

---

Thus prompt cards are meant as reminders and not arm-twisters.

When compiling a check-list, only use comparable items. Clear instructions should say if only one item or all relevant items can be recorded. Furthermore, you must be consistent as to whether the interviewer or the respondent reads the list.

## Some worked examples in the choice of answer system

For each example state everything you think is wrong with the choice of answer system offered.

---

1  Which of these apply to you?

|  |  |
|---|---|
|  | Married    1 |
| PASS CARD TO RESPONDENT SHOWING: | Single     2 |
| MARRIED, SINGLE, WIDOWED, DIVORCED, | Widowed  3 |
| SEPARATED | Divorced  4 |
|  | Separated 4 |
| CODE REPLIES |  |

---

Criticisms include: Does married mean married 'now'? What about unmarried couple/partners? All could apply but question unclear in this respect. Why distinguish between widowed, divorced and separated? Code numbers suggest categories are somehow ranked. Same code number for divorced and separated suggest they are the same. Clearly, the need for a question such as this will depend on the survey topic.

---

2  Generally speaking, how much trust do you have in the claims made about holiday products in television advertising? SHOW CARD AND CODE REPLIES

1    2    3    4    5    6    7    8    9    10
NONE AT ALL                          A GREAT DEAL

NUMBER ..........

---

Criticisms include: No explanation of how to use answer system. Unclear whether a score of 1, 2 and 3 refer to 'none at all'. What if the respondent is unsure or undecided? It could be argued that the scale is too wide.

3 What is your opinion of the holiday brochure I left you to read?

READ OUT THE SIX CHOICES TO THE RESPONDENT. REVERSE THE ORDER OF READ OUT IN GOING FROM ONE RESPONDENT TO THE NEXT.

| | |
|---|---|
| Extremely good | 1 |
| Very good | 2 |
| Fairly good | 3 |
| Not so good | 4 |
| Pretty poor | 5 |
| Awful | 6 |
| No opinion | 7 |

Criticisms include: Respondent may not be able to hold all seven in mind whilst making a choice. Scale is biased. Interviewer may be tempted into using scale as a running prompt (i.e. reading out scale slowly and stopping after respondent indicates a suitable choice). May not be able to rely on an interviewer to alternate (if this is determined as important (which in itself is questionable) different questionnaires should be provided).

4 Last week, did you work ......

CALL OUT FOLLOWING, CODING AS YOU GO.

| | |
|---|---|
| For an employer for wages, salary, payment in kind, etc. | 1 |
| In your own business with employees | 2 |
| In your own business, no employees | 3 |
| Without pay in family business | 4 |

Criticisms include: Choices may not fit all categories. What does 'etc.' mean? Respondent may not have worked last week but be in employment.

## Summary

Designing a questionnaire is clearly a crucial part of the market research process. Questionnaires are used in different types of survey from the highly structured commonly used in street and postal surveys to the informal where interviewers may ask open questions requiring in-depth answers. Whatever the purpose of the survey, the main aims of the questionnaire are to:

- obtain accurate information from the respondent;
- provide a structure and format to an interview;
- facilitate data analysis.

The chapter has demonstrated important considerations to be remembered when framing questions and laying out the questionnaire. Of particular importance in asking questions is the need to be clear and simple and to avoid bias which occurs when questions are leading, hypothetical or ambiguous.

It should also be stressed that the testing of questions within pilot surveys is critical. This will show up problems of understanding and misinterpretation and give some indications of the likely results. On this latter point it should be borne in mind that it is possible (and probable) that you will achieve different results when asking the same question but using open rather than closed techniques. For example, an open question asking 'What did you like about your last holiday?' would probably provide a wide range of answers which reflected that respondent's own particular circumstances and experiences. If, however, the question was asked in a closed type, such as 'The following list shows things which people often like about their holidays. Which are true about your last holiday?' Here the questions are trying to achive the same objective but the responses will be quite dissimilar. The open question may provide a wider range but will be more difficult to analyse, whereas the closed question may provide a narrower range of responses (depending on how many items are on the list) but will be easier to analyse. What could be lost in the closed question are items that respondents would have stated were important but not on the list. Equally with the open question, respondents may not remember things which were important at the time (which a checklist might prompt) but are forgotten when interviewed.

Unfortunately for the researcher, there is necessarily no absolute right or wrong approach. The best solution, perhaps, is to reflect on the objectives of the survey and include more than one questioning technique for each specific research objective. This way the pros and cons of question types will be compensated and a full response will be provided over all.

# Exercise: questionnaire design critique

## Brief

You have recently been employed by Leisure Consultants Ltd, who carry out consultancy in the leisure, recreation and tourism field. The company has just landed a contract to undertake market research for a conglomerate which has some interests in tourism facilities in the UK. One aspect of this contract (a fairly minor one) is to evaluate the future use of a zoo and wildlife park. There are several aspects to this contract including a feasibility study and a visitor survey of current visitors. It is this latter aspect that your boss has delegated to you. The deadline is tight and without visiting the site she (your boss) needs a report on how the company should go about undertaking the visitor survey. There is no time for you to visit the site, nor talk to anybody who has worked there. Thus at this stage she needs a report on what you feel would be a suitable method of undertaking a visitor survey, how long it should take and how much it would cost. To help (or hinder you) your boss has given you a questionnaire from a similar survey which she conducted elsewhere some years ago.

## Facts

- The wildlife park is called Tiptree Zoo, and is based in South Devon between Ashburton and Buckfastleigh.
- It currently has 35 000 visitors a year on a 250 acre site, with an adult charge £5 and children under 16, £2.50.
- On the site there are four main sections: animals, reptiles, birds and fish.
- In addition there is a gift shop, catering kiosk, cafeteria, children's play area, and interpretation provision. This consists of leaflets to guide visitors around the zoo itself, and displays in a wildlife interpretation centre.

## Objectives of your visitor survey

To establish:

1 Characteristics of current visitors, who they are, where they come from, and any other variables you consider suitable for comparative purposes.
2 Their past and current day trip activities.
3 Their use of Tiptree Zoo and their opinions towards current aspects of it.

## What you have to do

1 Criticize the existing questionnaire and state all that you consider to be wrong with it, both in terms of what is presented and the approach that was adopted. To this end you may have to make deductions about aspects that are not immediately apparent.
2 Write a report indicating how you would satisfy the brief given. The report should include an identification of the necessary planning stages, and reference to the investigatory, analysis and write up stages.

In short you need to design a suitable approach and include aspects such as methods, sampling, population and sample identification, fieldwork, analysis requirements and proposed budget. On this latter point no budget has been set and your boss has indicated that she would like you to prepare and justify what you need to do the job properly. If what you propose is not feasible within the context of the objectives you can expect the supervision of the contract to be passed to your main competitor in the department and you will end up being an interviewer and doing the coding!

This is the questionnaire designed by your boss for criticism. The method for this visitor survey was an on-site face-to-face method of data collection. No other techniques were used.

# Wickham Zoo Survey 1978

Ensure you have the letter of authority from the zoo with you in case it is required.

Good morning/afternoon. I would like to ask you a few questions about the zoo. Could you help me complete this questionnaire ?

Time ............. Date ........... Weather ...........................

Code No. ...............

1  INTERVIEWER CODE GENDER
   Male .........   Female .........

2  Is this your first visit to Wickham Zoo?
   Yes .........   No .........

3  How many times have you visited the zoo in the last ten years?
   Once .... Twice .... 3–4 times .... 5 or over ....

4  Was your last visit in the past
   3 months .... 6 months ....
   1 year .... Over 1 year ....

5  Have you been to another zoo or day trip attraction in the last 5 years?
   Yes .........   No .........

6  How does Wickham Zoo compare to the last one visited ?
   Much better                              Much worse
   1    2    3    4    5    6    7    8    9    10

7  Who have you come with today?
   INTERVIEWER TO ESTABLISH GROUP AND RECORD BELOW
   .........................................................................

8   How long have you spent at the zoo today?
Up to 1 hour .........     1-2 hours .........
3-4 hours .........     Over 4 hours .........

9   When did you decide to come here today? READ OUT
Today .........     In the past week .........
Longer .........     Don't know .........

10  Why did you decide to come here today ?
For educational purposes ....
For the children ....
To be entertained ....

11  How did you get to the site here today on your visit?
Foot ....   Car ....   Van ....   Motor bike ....
Bus ....   Bicycle ....   Coach ....   Train ....

12  Have you
Come from home ......
On holiday in the Wickham area .......

13  What accommodation are you staying in?
RECORD ANSWER
............................................................................

14  How long did it take you to get here today?
RECORD ANSWER
............................................................................

15  Many people come here on recommendation of their
friends. How did you hear about the site?
RECORD ANSWER
............................................................................

16  When you entered the zoo did you pay the full price
or the discounted price that is on offer today?
Full price .........     Discount .........

17  How would you rate the following aspects of the site?

|  | Good | Average | Poor | Very poor | Don't know |
|---|---|---|---|---|---|
| Animals |  |  |  |  |  |
| Reptiles |  |  |  |  |  |
| Birds |  |  |  |  |  |
| Fish |  |  |  |  |  |
| Viewing arrangements |  |  |  |  |  |
| Car park |  |  |  |  |  |
| Toilets |  |  |  |  |  |
| Catering |  |  |  |  |  |
| Admission charges |  |  |  |  |  |
| Staff courtesy |  |  |  |  |  |

18  Do you think that the facilities are adequate?
    Yes ......... No .........

19  Do you think we should provide additional facilities?
    Yes ......... No .........

20  Do you think additional facilities would spoil the look of the site?
    yes      1       2       3       4       5       no

21a Don't you think there should be more catering facilities and toilets?
    Yes .... No .... Don't know .... Undecided ....

21b Why is that? RECORD BELOW
    ............................................................................

22  We find that the most of our customers spend in excess of ten pounds, not including the entrance charge. How much did you spend?

|  | Up to £1 | £1–5 | £5–10 | £10+ |
|---|---|---|---|---|
| Catering |  |  |  |  |
| Shops |  |  |  |  |
| Kiosk |  |  |  |  |
| Total spent per person |  |  |  |  |

23a Are you satisfied with your purchases?
Yes ………   No ………
Don't know ………   Undecided ………

23b Why is that? RECORD BELOW

……………………………………………………………………………

24  What did you like about the zoo least?
RECORD BELOW

……………………………………………………………………………

25  Most people like the animals most. What did you like? RECORD BELOW

……………………………………………………………………………

26  Which category best describes your age?
12-16      16-20      21-25      26-34      35-44
45-54      55-64      65+

27  What is the occupational class of the head of the household?
A    B    C1    C2    D    E    Unemployed
OTHER

28  Finally, what is your address?
Address……………………………………………………………………
Town………………………………………………………………………
County……………………………………………………………………

# Further reading

Hague, P. (1993). *Questionnaire design*. London: Kogan Page.

This book covers all aspects of questionnaire design from deciding what type of questionnaire to use through to framing questions, laying out a questionnaire and instructions for interviewers. It provides examples from the general field of business and management.

Moser, Sir C.A. and Kalton, G. (1993). *Survey methods in social investigation*. Second edition. London: Heinemann.

Three chapters of this book are specifically dedicated to aspects relating to questionnaire design. These include the general principles of questionnaire design, scaling methods and errors found in responses.

Oppenheim, A.N. (1992). *Questionnaire design and attitude measurement*. Second edition. London: Heinemann.

The first edition of this book was published in 1966 and it has been in print since that time. Whilst it is a general book on questionnaire design using wide ranging examples from different fields, the student of travel and tourism will find many useful ideas and references. There are chapters devoted to the wording of questions, checklists, attitude questions and other types of questioning techniques.

| 6 | *Collecting the data* |

## Learning objectives

- To appreciate the interviewing requirements of different methods of data collection.
- To understand the stages involved in planning an interview survey.
- To be able to identify the do's and don'ts of interviewing.
- To appraise different interviewing techniques.
- Common errors with interviews.

## 6.1 Introduction

During the length of a project fieldwork is carried out at various times. The nature of the fieldwork depends upon the type of project and methods of data collection. If a survey is to be carried out at a tourist attraction then it will be necessary to first gain an overview of the site, decide upon suitable interviewing points and talk to staff to gain an understanding of the patterns of site use. There may also be fieldwork involved with observations of visitors either as part of the data collection process or to assist in developing a sampling frame.

When it comes to the actual data collection itself, there is a variety of aspects which need to be planned. This chapter is essentially divided into two parts. The first part will look at the arrangements which are required for data collection (subdivided by the main methods of data collection). The second part focusses on the nature and practice of undertaking interviews.

## 6.2 Data collection arrangements

### Postal and other self-completion surveys

In Chapter 2 the various advantages of self-completion surveys were discussed. Assuming that a postal survey has been decided upon, then consideration needs to be given to how the survey will be conducted to achieve the best possible response rate. When sending out questionnaires by post, attention should be paid to:

### 1 *The covering letter*

Often a letter accompanies the questionnaire and aims to get the recipient to take part in the survey. If possible, the more 'personal' this can be the better. An individual's name rather than 'Dear Sir/Madam' (or, even worse, 'The Occupier') is more likely to catch attention. The letter should introduce the purpose of the survey and stress the confidentiality of the respondents.

The covering letter should also explain who is sponsoring the research. In the author's experience students explaining that their research is properly supervised and endorsed by their tutor can achieve high response rates. This is because well written covering letters explaining, truthfully, that the project will help with the student's educational advancement can go far in appealing to the respondent's altruistic sentiments.

### 2 *The questionnaire*

As mentioned previously, self-completion surveys may be seen to have the particular disadvantage that no interviewer is present to explain and prompt. Thus the questionnaire layout and presentation require greater consideration than for surveys where an interviewer conducts the data collection. In this latter case, interviewers can be trained and can practise using the questionnaire; this is not so for respondents on their own. Research has been undertaken to test what types of format, fonts, colour and length are best. Clearly, the nature of the project and available budget may determine these factors. The main consideration is that the questionnaire must be clear, easy to understand and as professionally laid out and printed as the budget permits.

*3  Method of postage*

One of the largest costs of postal surveys is the postage to respondents and where a postal reply envelope is provided. Pre-paid (Freepost) labels are a satisfactory method as only those returned are chargeable. However, there is some suggestion (Frankfort-Nachmias and Nachmias, 1992) that such business-reply envelopes achieve slightly lower response rates than those where a normal stamp is attached.

*4  Reminders*

After the first distribution of questionnaires, reminders are often required to boost the response rates. Obviously extra cost is involved here and requires the researcher to be able to identify which respondents have not replied. When contemplating this method of data collection, the time involved following up late responders should be anticipated as it can lengthen the whole data collection period. Some researchers include a gift or entry into a free draw as an inducement to participate. However, care should be taken not to offend particular respondents who would be willing to take part anyway because of the value of the survey. Monetary or other inducements perhaps suggest that a low response rate is already anticipated.

Overall, the various stages involved with the data collection of postal surveys are as follows:

| | | |
|---|---|---|
| i | Questionnaire preparation | presentation layout printing |
| ii | Covering letter | presentation layout printing |
| iii | Postage preparation | filling envelopes addressing |
| iv | First reminder postage | decision whether to include questionnaire and reply envelope or just letter |
| v | Subsequent reminders | as necessary within time and budget |

## Surveys with interviewers

With many surveys staff are required to perform the data collection. This may be the actual interviews with respondents, undertaking observations or manually recording tourist numbers. Once the sampling frame has been developed and the questionnaire designed and tested, the precise staffing requirements can be calculated. Where interviewers are used to collect the data, several factors require thought, as follows:

### 1 Recruitment of interviewers

Skilful interviewing is not within everyone's capabilities. Interviewers need to be able to probe answers, have administrative ability and be able to stay strictly within whatever sampling or interview instructions are required. In addition, interviewers must be able to approach all types of people and gain their cooperation. Perhaps of most importance is that the potential interviewer should enjoy interviewing.

Depending upon the nature and timing of the research, students are sometimes used because of their availability in the summer months. However, it is essential that younger people possess the right personality and confidence to interview older members of the public, particularly in relation to questions regarding income. Larger organizations and market research companies often have a pool of experienced staff to whom they turn for interviewing. In the case of in-depth, qualitative interviews and focus groups, prior experience is essential.

### 2 Training interviewers

All interviewers whether new or experienced should be briefed on the particular requirements of the project. The nature of the training may take a variety of forms, but commonly includes:

a  An instruction manual. This outlines the purpose of the survey, interview techniques, questionnaire, sampling instructions and any other relevant guidelines.
b  In-class training. Interviewers are brought together for instruction on survey requirements.
c  Field training. As above, but also including supervised training and practice in the field prior to the main survey.

Often one of the interviewers is appointed as a supervisor. His or her particular responsibilities will involve dealing with problems that invariably occur on the first day, checking the quality of the interviews and ensuring that all information is accurately recorded. Overall there are some general guidelines which interviewers must learn and adhere to (though variations may occur for particular surveys).

**THINGS INTERVIEWERS MUST *ALWAYS DO***

1   Be courteous, confident and positive.
2   Follow all instructions closely.
3   Practise interviewing prior to data collection.
4   Make sure that all necessary materials are carried (prompt cards, identity card, questionnaires, pens, clip board, etc).
5   Be smartly dressed.
6   Interview respondents on their own (unless couples or groups are specified).
7   Outline the introduction correctly (explaining the purpose of the survey, for whom, by whom, and assure confidentiality).
8   Ask questions in the correct order.
9   Ask all the appropriate questions.
10  Record the answers fully and accurately.
11  Thank the respondent for their cooperation.

**THINGS INTERVIEWERS MUST *NEVER DO***

1   Mislead respondents about the length of the interview.
2   Chat about other issues.
3   Pass any opinion about respondents' answers.
4   Allow the respondent to see the questionnaire.
5   Interview people personally known (occasionally this may be unavoidable).
6   Interview people previously interviewed on another survey day.
7   Interview children without appropriate permission.
8   Interview as tourists people who work at the site.

### 3 Payment of interviewers

In the training of interviewers time should be spent ensuring that the methods of payment (including travel and subsistence expenses) are thoroughly understood. This is especially the case where temporary staff are employed for the data collection. Clearly the level of payment is determined by the budget or organization but should reflect a level well above basic clerical staff and take account of the sometimes arduous working conditions. Payment should be promptly made, again particularly for temporary staff who may have limited funds to cope with legitimate expenses before their first payment is received.

## 6.3 Interviewing

This section is divided into four parts investigating the nature and practice of undertaking interviews. The first part discusses the different types of interview followed by interview errors, telephone and group interviews.

### Types of interview

When interviewing individual respondents there are perhaps two broad types of interview method, structured and unstructured. The differences between them are revealed in Table 6.1.

Between these two extremes are a variety of other techniques which are more or less structured. For example, some interviews avoid a standardized questionnaire but answers are 'focussed' around a series of open questions which gently guide the respondent. On the other hand, where there is unsystematic questioning of respondents, only a topic area may be specified by the interviewer and the respondent is free to pursue his/her own particular line of thought.

Whilst it may appear easy to be dismissive of unstructured interviews as a waste of time, the purpose of the two broad methods should be considered. Unstructured interviews may be used to 'discover' the attitudes and opinions of, say, a tourist rather than to 'prove' or 'test' something. If the research objective is to test whether age or social class has an influence on tourist purchasing behaviour, then something more structured will be necessary. However, in doing so it may be first appropriate to discover the range of views with unstructured interviews so that a structured questionnaire and interviews can be designed and conducted. Hence, unstructured (or less structured) interviews may be useful in the preliminary stages in preparing for and informing more structured data collection.

**Table 6.1** *Comparison of interview types*

| Type | Structured interviews | Unstructured interviews |
|---|---|---|
| Other words to describe | Formal, guided, systematic. | Informal, less or unguided, unsystematic. |
| Interview questions | Determined prior to interview, often standardized on questionnaire. Sequence and interviewer instruction strictly controlled. | May have no set questions but topics raised/covered as appropriate to respondent. |
| Conversation | Very unlike a natural conversation as highly systematic. | More like an informal conversation. |
| Probing | Limited to open questions geared to gaining full response to question. | Highly important. Respondents free to answer, probing used to develop deeper understanding. |
| Advantages | Comparability of answers lends itself to quantitative analysis. | 'Rich' information, greater likelihood of respondents revealing more opinions/attitudes. |
| Disadvantages | Loss of spontaneity/depth of response. | Difficulty of comparison in quantitative terms. |

## Common errors in interviews

Errors can occur throughout the survey process. Chapter 5 suggested how questions can be poorly written, which leads to error in terms of inaccurate or poor responses. Chapter 4 highlighted potential pitfalls with sampling, which again can lead to unrepresentative results occurring. Moreover, the correct selection of the method of data collection for the purpose of the market research is crucial to the success of the project. When it comes to interviewing, there are, again, several areas where errors can occur. These are now discussed.

### 1 Interviewer cheating

Perhaps the most dramatic of all interview errors is cheating by the interviewer. The worst form of this is the falsification of data, that is, making up the responses. Either fictitious respondents who were never interviewed are recorded or not all the interview was completed and the interviewer 'makes up' the gaps. In either case the action is deliberate and dishonest. To control and discourage this, the research director must put in place a variety of checks upon the interviewers. For site surveys at tourist attractions the interviewer can be observed periodically and his/her questionnaires checked throughout the day. For interviews in the respondent's home, where names and addresses are required, interviewers can explain that a small sub-sample of respondents will be contacted to verify that an interview took place. Such checks can avoid this type of problem arising.

### 2 Interviewer influence: Type 1

Occasionally, in an attempt to develop a rapport with the respondent, or because the interviewer is embarrassed asking certain questions, the interviewer will pass a personal opinion. Where this happens, bias may be introduced into the responses. A respondent may not wish to disagree with the interviewer or be uncertain about their own opinion and consequently 'side' with the interviewer. Such bias is clearly inappropriate and should be a focus of training in the survey requirements. Regardless of the nature of the research or interview technique, the interviewer must never pass their own opinion.

### 3 Interviewer influence: Type 2

Another type of interviewer bias occurs in relation to the appearance and unspoken manner of the interviewer when interacting with the respondent. Age, gender, apparent class, ethnic origin, personality, clothes, hair style may all have some influence on how respondents react. Similarly, the age, gender, etc., of the respondent may in turn affect the interviewer's approach. In western countries, women are often more successful as interviewers, particularly where it is necessary to gain entry into households to collect data. Day-time home-based interviews of females by male interviewers may inevitably suffer from low response rates. In very large surveys these influences may be limited, but how a potential interviewer will be viewed by respondents should be given consideration in the selection procedure.

## 4 Errors when asking questions

Sometimes, quite unwittingly and with the best intentions, interviewers will change the wording of a question. This may be done to better fit the way the interviewer would ask such a question or be reworded thinking it would elicit a better reply from the respondent. In structured interviews such practice cannot be permitted, as considerable variability in the responses may occur. In the author's own experience (Brunt, 1990) where a face-to-face site survey of a tourist attraction was being undertaken, an open question required respondents to state where they had been on day trips in the previous four weeks. For speed of coding, a range of different types of day trip site were printed on the questionnaire for the interviewers' own use. Because it was a difficult question, requiring recall, one interviewer speeded up the process by using the questionnaire as a prompt card and asked respondent to indicate yes or no to each of the categories printed on it. Consequently, the results from this interviewer were completely out of step with other interviewers who asked the question in the way intended. This type of problem, yet again, stresses the need for clear instructions and thorough training.

## 5 Problems with probing

Even structured questionnaires often have a number of 'open' questions where interviewers must 'probe' for the fullest possible answer. However, where several interviewers are used to collect data there is a real possibility of inconsistency between them. Clearly, where the aim of the survey is to compare the responses to such questions and make judgements, inconsistent answers from variable probing are worthless. To cope with this type of problem, there are a variety of solutions, as listed below:

- Extensive interviewer training.
- A probing 'pro-forma', i.e. probing on strictly prescribed lines.
- Mixture of question types. Open questions followed by closed questions of the same topic to facilitate cross checking.

- No open questions at all.
- Separate data collection method using unstructured interviews in support of structured ones.

### 6 *Errors recording the answers*

With closed questions where the interviewer is required to tick a box, errors here are down to carelessness. This of course assumes the interviewer understands how to complete the questionnaire. Other errors of this type occur in response to open questions where either the interviewer must write down what is said or interpret the open answer and allocate it to a particular box of pre-coded categories. The potential for error in the former case is due to carelessness, laziness in writing or trying to abbreviate the answer and in doing so missing the point. In the latter case, interpretation of replies and trying to make them 'fit' a particular category can cause bias. Wherever such circumstances arise, it is better for interviewers to record answers verbatim, as opposed to paraphrasing or only writing down what appears relevant. For interviewers to listen, interpret and then write an answer down in brief whilst maintaining rapport is difficult. Accuracy and consistency can be easily lost. It is preferable for interpretation to occur at a later stage. This solution further avoids potential problems by variability between interviewers in terms of their vocabulary and ability to summarize.

## Telephone interviews

Telephones have become a part of everyday life and as such now provide the researcher with a convenient, cost effective method of conducting an interview. This has not always been the case. In the 1950s and 1960s, fewer people owned or had access to a telephone and hence this method tended to result in a sample biased towards more affluent people. Nowadays this is much less the case. Moreover, it could be argued that in the field of travel and tourism very few respondents who are able to afford a holiday are unlikely not to own a telephone. The telephone is useful for arranging appointments for a personal interview, checking that personal interviews have been carried out and for reminders with postal surveys.

The telephone interview has the advantage of reduced cost, with savings on travel for personal interviews being the main area.

It also provides a speedy method of data collection. Interviewers can code and input the data directly into computers whilst the interview is progressing. In addition, the interview supervisor is able to listen to interviewers to ensure that questions are correctly asked and coded.

There are some disadvantages though. As an alternative to personal interviews the telephone is more impersonal and respondents may break off the interview easily. The use of checklists and prompt cards is severely limited and thus the ability to gain detailed information is less than for personal interviews. In addition to the normal requirements, interviewers need to have a clear voice, and an easy-to-understand accent.

## Group interviews

Group interviews involve a recorded discussion of perhaps ten people who share a common interest (such as having undertaken the same holiday). Open questions are asked of the group and the interviewer acts as a discussion leader. The main functions other than this of the leader are to ensure that the discussion does not stray from the topic in hand by occasionally prompting, and to ensure that all members have an equal opportunity to speak.

Group interviews are useful to gain an understanding of 'why' particular behaviour occurred. In tourism, this can be most useful to find out what motivates travel to particular destinations. The information collected in this way is often detailed and lengthy. Thus group interviews are particularly valuable in the exploratory stages of research or to provide qualitative information alongside a quantitative survey. When developing the group interview method, the following list provides some practical considerations.

| | | |
|---|---|---|
| 1 | *The leader* | Must have thorough training and experience. |
| 2 | *The location* | Must be appropriate for the respondents who will make up the group. Thus, a back room of a public house, hotel or church hall might be suitable for resort guest house owners, marketing managers of airlines and touring caravan owners respectively. |
| 3 | *Number of respondents* | Eight to ten is ideal as larger than this may be unmanageable in terms of letting everyone have an equal input. |

| | |
|---|---|
| 4 *Timing* | To ensure a respectable response rate, select a time when respondents are most likely to be available. |
| 5 *Recording* | Tape recording is easiest. Video recording may provide additional insights into the dynamics of the group. The main consideration is that the recording equipment must be quiet and unobtrusive. |
| 6 *Respondent type* | Respondents should share a common interest related to the topic of the research. There should be balance within the group in terms of gender, age or other characteristics (e.g. buying behaviour). Some groups may be made up of particular types (e.g. all male) but effort should be made to avoid a single individual differing significantly in some way from the rest of the group. If possible, respondents should not know each other or have had previous experience of this type of research. |
| 7 *Refreshments* | When respondents arrive they should be welcomed and helped to relax. Refreshments can be served and respondents can get to know each other informally. |
| 8 *Questions* | The leader opens the discussion with some general questions and explanation of how the discussion will be run. From this point on the leader takes a 'back seat' role unless:<br>• one person dominates the discussion (must be suppressed);<br>• a respondent is not taking part (question should be specifically directed);<br>• a respondent is aggressive/ unhelpful (reason for aggression probed and encouraged to participate positively). |
| 9 *Silences* | These can be embarrassing, but leader should resist stepping in unless absolutely necessary. Pauses can prompt respondents to become involved with comments that have been carefully thought out. |

Overall, group interviews can yield large amounts of valuable qualitative data. The results come not only from what was said by members of the group but also from the interaction within the group. Where it is important to investigate the reason for behaviour, group interviews can be most useful, especially in the exploratory stages of the project.

# Case study

To illustrate the do's and don'ts of interviewing, the following is an example of some initial questions of a site visitor survey. Whilst the transcripts are clearly hypothetical, the questions are selected from a questionnaire which was used by the author in a consultancy contract.

### Interview A

### Interviewer A
Good morning, sir. I am carrying out a survey on behalf of Torbay Borough Council to find out your views of Cockington Country Park. Would you please help us by answering a few strictly confidential questions which will take no more than ten minutes?

### Respondent A
OK, you can ask me.

### Question 1
*Where have you come from today?* (Instructions are to allow respondent to answer and simply code within or outside Torbay)
### Respondent A
I've come from Paignton today (within Torbay).

### Question 2
*Is that your home or are you on holiday?*
### Respondent A
I am on holiday at the moment with my family.

### Question 3
*What is the purpose of your visit here today?* (Instructions to the interviewer are to allow the respondent to answer freely and probe for a full answer).

**Respondent A**
Well as I said we're on holiday and we decided to have a day away from the beach.

**Interviewer A**
Uh-huh.
**Respondent A**
Oh, and we saw this place advertised in the hotel, so we thought we'd give it a try.

**Interviewer A**
That's interesting was there anything else which was important?
**Respondent A**
Well yes, the kids liked the idea of a horse and cart ride and we decided to have a family treat here with a picnic and ride back to the sea front.

**Question 4a**
*Have you ever been to Cockington before?* (This is a filter question, if the respondent indicates that they had been before, 4b asks how often they visit Cockington and a prompt card is issued showing categories, e.g. daily, weekly, fortnightly, etc.).
**Respondent A**
No this is our first visit.

*Interview continues successfully*


**Interview B**

**Interviewer B**
Hello, folks, we're doing a survey. Can you answer a few questions?
**Respondents B**
Well we all liked our visit, didn't we, yes I suppose we can answer a few questions if it's not too long.

**Question 1**
*Where have you 'all' come from today?* (Instructions are to allow respondent to answer and simply code within or outside Torbay)
**Respondents B**
We have all come from Paignton this morning.

## Question 2
*Is that your home or are you on holiday?*
### Respondents B
Well my wife and I live there and this couple are our friends who are on holiday staying with us. We've been here lots of times but this is their first visit. ... No it isn't. We came years ago before it was all developed and you just had to walk across the fields...Well it must have been before we were married, Frank, because I'm sure I've never been here before... Well I'm sure I have, the cottages must have been there then though, but I don't remember seeing them ... yes they're very pretty, but you can't go in them ... No it's a shame you can't look inside. Is that because people live there ... Yes ... anyway we're not helping this nice young man. What is your next question? Only you will have to be quick because I haven't much time left on the car park ticket and if we're going to get a good seat at the pub for lunch in Babbacombe we'll have to get a move on.

### Interviewer B
I'll only be a couple of minutes so you'll be OK in the car park. The traffic warden hasn't been around today. Look I have to have one of you as my respondent or we'll get in a terrible muddle ...
### Respondents B
Well you've been here the most, George. You had better answer his questions.

### Interviewer B
That's fine, so you have come from your home today.
### Resp. B (George)
Yes, are there many more questions?
### Interviewer B
No, just a few.

## Question 3
*What is the purpose of your visit here today?* (Instructions to the interviewer are to allow the respondent to answer freely and probe for a full answer).
### Resp. B (George)
Well like we said we had our visitors staying and decided to show them somewhere, where I thought they hadn't been before.

**Interviewer B**

Thanks, the next questions asks …

**Resp. B (George)**

Look I'd better go and get the car. Frank can answer the rest of your questions and I'll pick you up when you finished.

## Question 4a

*Have you ever been to Cockington before?* (This is a filter question. If the respondent indicates that they had been before, 4b asks how often they visit Cockington and a prompt card is issued showing categories e.g. daily, weekly, fortnightly, etc.).

**Resp. B (Frank)**

Yes, though my wife thinks I haven't. George and Mary come here a lot, but then they live close by.

**Interviewer B**

Look at this card, which of the categories best explains how often you visit Cockington?

**Resp. B (Frank)**

Well I just said I have been here once before, oh it must have been forty years ago. You don't really have a category for that, why don't I answer for George and Mary, I'm sure they must come here every week.

*George and Mary arrive in the car and off they all go to Babbacombe for lunch. The interview was not completed. Interviewer B looks around to see if the supervisor was watching and thinks about filling in the rest of the questionnaire himself. To make matters worse Interviewer A has finished for the day. B thinks there must be an easier way to earn a living. Perhaps I'll become a traffic warden.*

## Comments

*Introduction*

Interviewer A asked the introduction which was printed on the questionnaire. As such she referred to the commissioning organization which is good for public relations, indicated that the responses would be confidential and how long the interview would take. B did not follow the instructions but made up his own introduction which, whilst he may have felt was quicker and more chatty, left the potential respondent without appropriate information on which to decide whether to take part in the survey or not. Because it was not the same as A and deviated from the instructions there may well have been differences in the response rates between A and B which could have a bearing on the sampling through interviewer bias.

### Response to introduction

While A gets a positive response immediately, B's respondent seems less sure, especially over how long it is going to take. Moreover, B should step in at this point and indicate that an individual respondent is required, as group responses may be confusing.

### Questions 1 and 2

The responses to A's questions are easy to understand and code. B, however, has not realized the importance of having only one respondent because the group are split over whether they have come from home or are on a holiday. B has not taken control of the interview as the responses show that while the group are trying to be helpful they are digressing from the questions. The way this is resolved is not particularly satisfactory as the group have self-selected their spokesperson. It is also clear that the respondent wants to get away and doesn't really have much time to answer the questions. This aspect would have been covered if B had read out the introduction properly so that the respondents may have politely declined if they were unable to answer questions for ten minutes.

### Question 3

Interviewer A asks the question properly. The first response is not complete so A makes a non-verbal response, gets some more information and then again encourages the respondent to develop the answer more fully. In the end the purpose of the visit is clear. B however senses the irritation and urgency of the respondent and does not bother to probe. Furthermore the interview is terminated by the respondent, George, and replaced by Frank. At this point B should realize his mistakes, thank the respondents, and cease the interview. However, he perseveres regardless.

*Question 4*

By this time Interviewer A is in her stride and a good rapport has developed with the respondent. She has control over the interview and the respondent is relaxed in his answers and is happy with the experience of being interviewed. Interviewer B however has completely failed, the answers have moved from George to Frank, and the muddle anticipated has definitely occurred. In the main the failure is down to initially misleading the respondent about the length of the interview, not taking control by specifying that a single respondent was required and not following the instructions correctly. Had the interview been completed, then the quality of the answers would have been poor.

## Summary

Interviewing is a skill which requires training and practice. This is the case whether the survey requires a formal interview with structured questions or an informal interview where there is little standardization. Where interviewers are recruited, the right sort of individual in terms of administrative skill and personality is needed, as is thorough training. Supervision and ongoing monitoring of interviewers are required to overcome some of the common errors that can occur. Overall, interviewing can be a highly successful and accurate method, which achieves high quality data, providing that interviewers have the necessary skills and sound judgement.

## Exercises

1 What are the main problems encountered when interviewing?
2 Devise a training pack for inexperienced interviewers who are to carry out face-to-face interviews at a local country park.
3 With a partner, practise interviewing, using the questionnaire at the end of Chapter 5. See if you can find any other mistakes that interviewers would come across.

# Further reading

Frey, J.H. and Oishi, S.M. (1995). *How to conduct interviews by telephone and in person*. London: Sage Publications.

This book covers a wide variety of aspects associated with interviews, covering the different types of interview and useful techniques to achieve accurate results.

Morse, J.M. (Ed.) (1994). *Critical issues in qualitative research methods*. London: Sage Publications.

Morse edits contributions on a variety of issues associated with qualitative research methods. In the context of this chapter there are interesting contributions by Carey on focus groups and from Hutchinson and Wilson regarding interviews.

Moser, Sir C.A. and Kalton, G. (1993). *Survey methods in social investigation*. Second edition. London: Heinemann.

This key text has been recommended after several chapters. In this context, Moser and Kalton provide a detailed chapter dedicated to the collection of information by interviews. Within it, both theory and practical advice are provided as well as information on the selection and training of interviewers.

| 7 | *Dealing with the data* |

## Learning objectives

- To appreciate the need for prior planning in the analysis stage.
- To understand some basic principles and techniques of quantitative data analysis.
- To understand some basic principles and techniques of qualitative data analysis.

## 7.1 Overview

In the field of market research in travel and tourism the analysis of data is clearly a crucial part. Business life generally involves the description, analysis and evaluation of words and numbers. This has given rise to a whole series of terms which include statistics, quantitative analysis, qualitative analysis, models, trends and forecasts. Some of these expressions are specific while others attempt to cover a wider range of applications. Take for example the term statistics. It could be easily argued that to the general public any numbers, facts and figures, graphs and tables are all statistics. However, statistics is also a subject or body of knowledge which statisticians use. Furthermore, statistics relate to specific calculations of quantities derived from sample data. In the context here the purpose is not to get too bogged down by terminology but to introduce enough to develop an understanding of a specific range of analytical techniques which the readership of this book can master and use.

Added to this is the world of computers. There are many sophisticated software packages for analysing both quantitative and qualitative data. It is beyond the scope of this book to select a particular package and explain how to use it, as such information is readily available elsewhere (and is referred to in the Further reading section at the end of this chapter). Using software to analyse data is clearly sensible and pragmatic but is only effective if the user has a thorough understanding of the basic analytical principles and techniques. Without this the individual researcher may well be able to get a software package to carry out a series of statistical tests but would be unable to properly interpret the results. This emphasizes the point that the analysing data is much more than a single stage or event in a project. Knowing why particular analytical techniques are appropriate, interpreting the results fully and suggesting or recommending a suitable course of action, are equally if not more important than performing a specific statistical test.

Chapter 3 indicated the need for consideration of the proposed analysis in the early planning stages of a project. It is easy to forget the importance of this aspect in the midst of a project when time pressures are forcing the researcher to get on with designing questionnaires and starting the data collection. Soon the data are collected, coded and perhaps put onto a spreadsheet. Suddenly the question arises 'what do I do now?' The answer is 'well analyse it.' However, in answer to 'what are you trying to achieve', there is often an embarrassing silence. In the planning stages of a project, where the aims and objectives are negotiated and agreed, thought must be given as to how the analysis will satisfy the objectives. Then, after the pilot stage, when some preliminary results are available, the question of whether the data can be analysed in the way proposed to satisfy the project objectives should be posed. In short, you should always try to anticipate how the analysis will be performed and ensure that the data collected are concordant with the proposed analysis and meet the requirements of the project objectives.

To address these issues this chapter is now divided into three parts:

- describing and illustrating data;
- quantitative analysis – focussing on the representation and analysis of quantitative data;
- qualitative analysis – focussing on the analysis of in-depth interviews and focus groups.

## 7.2 Describing and illustrating data

### Types of data

Quantitative data originate from a variety of different sources. These include surveys, measurements, government statistics and other secondary sources. Quantitative data can be one of three basic types:

Type 1   Categorical (sometimes also called nominal)
Type 2   Ordinal
Type 3   Cardinal (sometimes also called numerical)

Categorical data come from, for example, questionnaires where the responses to questions are put into classes, groups or categories. As such the data do not have a numerical value; rather, they have a label or value assigned to each category. Hence some authors (Fink, 1995) refer to this type of data as nominal. Some examples of questions resulting in categorical data are shown below.

---

Question 1   How did you travel to this site today? (tick one box)

Car (1)     ☐     Coach (2)   ☐   Service bus (3) ☐
Bicycle (4) ☐     Walked (5)  ☐   Other (6)       ☐

Question 2  Are you .......   1   Male   (circle as appropriate)
                              2   Female

---

As can be seen from the examples, the respondent indicates which category is relevant to them. In the case of gender or other questions where there are only two alternatives (yes or no questions for example), the data can be referred to as dichotomous.

Ordinal data are arranged in a specific order. The data are still arranged in categories but they must ascend or descend, for example go from best to worst or worst to best. Typically questions which use ranking scales produce ordinal data. In a similar way to categorical data it is not possible to measure precisely how much better one category is over another, other than that one category is higher in the order. The following examples illustrate the types of question which result in ordinal data.

**Question 3** Which of the statements best reflects your opinion of your experience with us.
Tick one box.

(i)   Staff anticipated all my requirements before I had to ask ☐

(ii)  Staff responded quickly to me and provided what I wanted ☐

(iii) Staff were slow to respond but did provide me with what I wanted ☐

(iv)  Staff were reluctant to respond and did not always provide me with what I wanted ☐

(v)   Staff did not always respond and/or did not provide me with what I wanted ☐

**Question 4** How would you rate the comfort of the aircraft seats?
(Use the following card and indicate a score where 1 means that you thought the seats provided excellent comfort down to 5 which means you thought the comfort of the seats was poor)

1    Excellent
2
3
4                    Score    ⬭
5    Poor

**Question 5** Indicate your level of agreement of the statements by ticking the appropriate box of whether you:   A   Agree strongly
                                          B   Agree
                                          C   Undecided
                                          D   Disagree
                                          E   Disagree strongly

| | A | B | C | D | E |
|---|---|---|---|---|---|
| I was satisfied with the standard of accommodation | ☐ | ☐ | ☐ | ☐ | ☐ |
| Staff were generally accessible and courteous | ☐ | ☐ | ☐ | ☐ | ☐ |
| I enjoyed the entertainment provided | ☐ | ☐ | ☐ | ☐ | ☐ |
| There was a wide range of food which suited all tastes | ☐ | ☐ | ☐ | ☐ | ☐ |

Cardinal data can be measured against a scale which has a specific numerical value. Thus, often the data can be reported in terms of measurable units, or else the data are an actual number. Hence, age in years, height in metres, cost in pounds, number of holidays taken, are all examples of cardinal data. In the last example where the amount would refer to a whole number or integer value, the data can also be referred to as discrete cardinal data. In the other examples such as height, age, cost, etc., where the answer could be any value, it is referred to as continuous cardinal data.

To summarize, data can be:
- **Categorical:** in categories, classes or groups
- **Ordinal:** categories put into some kind of rank order
- **Cardinal:** measurable against a scale and subdivided into:
  - discrete
  - continuous

## Variables, values and cases

Often in surveys the term **variable** is used to define an aspect or question which is measured. You may have asked respondents to state their age, number of children, number of holidays taken, and views of particular aspects of their last holiday. The question posed can be referred to as a **variable** and the answer given a **value**. In addition, each person (or sampling unit) can be defined as a **case**. Hence, as Norusis (1990) states 'for each case you have one value for each variable.'

Variables may be sub-divided between **independent** and **dependent**. This relates to the influence which a variable may have within the analysis. It is common to predict that variables such as age, presence of children, income, educational background, social class or gender may influence (or explain) the responses to other variables such as preferred holiday type, satisfaction with accommodation, type of transport used, purchasing behaviour or likelihood to repeat the visit. In this sense it could be said that the latter variables mentioned depend on the former ones. Hence:

- **Independent variables** are likely to be influential in predicting or explaining things. They act independently in the sense that the respondent has little control over the answer. For instance a respondent is female, with two children, aged 35, with a particular income, etc.
- **Dependent variables** refer to questions or variables where the respondent is more likely to indicate their feelings or opinions. Dependent variables are usually influenced by one or more variables which may control or relate to it.

It is very often the purpose of market research to find out 'why' certain types of customer are more or less likely to demonstrate particular types of purchasing behaviour. That is, 'who is most likely to want this type of tourism product?' Finding this out to inform a marketing strategy is the obvious and immediate function of market research. Thus, being able to distinguish which independent variables are significant in predicting favourable purchasing characteristics (dependent variables) is a priority.

### Reporting and illustrating data

When reporting the results of data collected it is important that the most effective way of conveying numerical information is considered. Often it is easier to explain such information in a diagram where the reader can visualize the result. Moreover, diagrams are more likely to both grasp attention and allow better interpretation than a page of numbers or solid text. Hence, the market researcher needs to be sensitive to the readership and report and represent the data in an attractive (and truthful) fashion. Whilst diagrams are useful, simple facts and figures often need to be reported and a decision has to be made whether to simply state the frequency, a proportion, percentage or ratio.

Stating a **frequency** may have little value other than, for instance, '1600 respondents satisfactorily completed the questionnaire'. To a knowledgeable audience this may have some meaning but out of context it is worthless. Thus often a **proportion** is used. Hence,

'1600 respondents satisfactorily completed the questionnaire from the 2500 that were distributed'. A proportion is therefore a section of the whole (or more accurately a section divided by the whole).

**Percentages** relate to a proportion multiplied by 100%. Thus, rather than saying 1600 out of 2500 completed their questionnaire, you could also state that 64% did so. This is calculated by 1600 divided by 2500 and then multiplied by 100. Another way of expressing numerical information is as a ratio. Using the same example you could state that the ratio of those completing their questionnaires to those who did not was 64 to 36 or 64/36.

The decision of whether to express results in terms of a frequency, proportion, percentage or ratio is largely up to the preference of the researcher, but it is important to be consistent. Consider the following statement:

*Of the 200 people interviewed at each of the four sites:*
- *40 people at the Butterfly Farm were from social class B*
- *20% of people at Lacy House were from social class B*
- *2 out of every 10 visitors to the Country Park were from social class B*
- *The ratio of those in social classes other than social class B was 10/2 at the Farm Museum.*

The statement is certainly confusing but it is an indication that exactly the same number of respondents at each of the four sites were found to be from social class B (40). This stresses the need to be consistent in discussing figures so that the reader can easily follow what is being explained. There is no right or wrong approach (although in the example the ratio expression is unnecessarily complicated). However, in this author's opinion expressing small proportions in terms of percentages sometimes appears to be a means of concealing a small sample size. For instance, say 12 sales managers had been interviewed about their ability to return their travel expenses on time. It was found that 7 of the 12 had met the deadline. Although factually correct, it would be unwise to state that 42% (rounded up) of sales managers did not meet the travel expenses deadline. Percentages should be used to simplify the readers' understanding. In this example it could be argued that using percentages confuses it.

To illustrate data in ways other than within text, tables and diagrams can be used. Perhaps the simplest method is to use a **frequency table** as illustrated in Table 7.1.

**Table** 7.1 *Method of travel to site*

|  | Frequency | Percentage |
|---|---|---|
| Car | 663 | 82.9 |
| Motorbike | 3 | 0.4 |
| Bicycle | 10 | 1.2 |
| Coach | 115 | 14.4 |
| Walked | 9 | 1.1 |
| Total | 800 | 100 |

Table 7.1 indicates how 'frequently' each of the responses occurs and the reader can see at a glance the results. By providing a percentage column the reader can also go further in judging the relative importance of each method of transport.

In this example the percentage given is the percentage of the total, but sometimes where filter questions are used this may include people who are not relevant. In this case it may be necessary to include columns in the table which demonstrate valid and cumulative percentages. Many computer packages perform this function by default. Table 7.2 gives an example.

**Table** 7.2 *Rating of improvements to facilities over the previous season.*

| Rating | Value | Frequency | Percentage | Valid % | Cumulative % |
|---|---|---|---|---|---|
| Excellent | 1 | 75 | 27.8 | 36.6 | 36.6 |
|  | 2 | 50 | 18.5 | 24.4 | 61.0 |
|  | 3 | 30 | 11.1 | 14.6 | 75.6 |
|  | 4 | 30 | 11.1 | 14.6 | 90.2 |
| Poor | 5 | 20 | 7.4 | 9.8 | 100 |
|  | 9 | 65 | 24.1 | Missing |  |
| Total |  | 270 | 100 | 100 |  |
| Valid cases |  | 205 | Missing cases | 65 |  |

In the example in Table 7.2 only 205 out of the 270 asked were able to answer the question and give a score of 1 to 5. These are noted below the table as the valid cases. The 65 missing cases coded as value 9 in the table were respondents who had not visited the site in the previous season and were therefore not asked this question. In these circumstances referring to a percentage of the whole sample (270) is misleading because of the 65 included who were unable to answer the question. Thus the **valid percentage** column is based on the percentage of those who were actually asked the question (205). In this way it can be seen that 75 people rated the improvements as excellent, which represents 27.8 per cent of all respondents or 36.6 per cent of those who were able to give an answer to this question. The final column, **cumulative percentage**, relates to the sum of the valid percentage for a response plus all the other responses that precede it in the table. Hence, 61 per cent of valid cases gave a score of 1 or 2 for the improvements to the facilities.

Whilst the tables in the examples given are straightforward, sometimes frequency tables can be difficult to interpret. In this instance, the researcher must consider how best to illustrate the data in the form of a diagram. The main methods include using **line graphs, bar charts, histograms and pie charts.** These will be discussed briefly followed by some examples.

Line graphs are useful for showing trends over time; data on the horizontal axis can be in numbers or categories, however data on the vertical axis must be represented by numbers. Because many points can be placed on a line graph, they are most valuable where a bar chart would appear too cluttered. Figure 7.1 illustrates the use of a line graph.

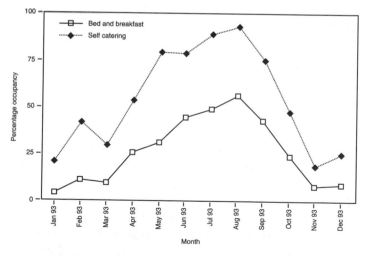

**Figure 7.1** *Example of a line graph*

Bar charts are mainly used for categorical data and also allow for comparisons between values. The length of a column in a bar chart is related to the number or frequency it represents. Hence, one of the columns must indicate a frequency, numerical value or percentage whilst the other axis will be the categories. There is no particular convention over whether the columns should be presented horizontally or vertically. However, if several bar charts are to be used in a report then a consistent approach is advisable. Figure 7.2 shows an example of a bar chart.

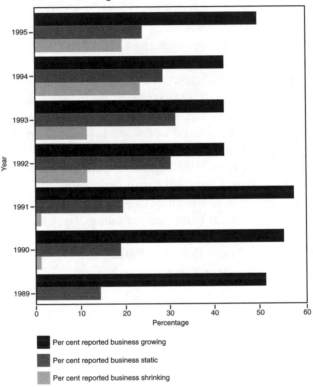

**Figure 7.2**  *Example of a bar chart*

Histograms are similar to bar charts, however histograms are more often used to illustrate cardinal (numerical) data such as age, sales, or income. Here, to construct a histogram it must be reasonable to combine adjacent values into columns to form the graph. Combining categorical data may not be possible as the categories may be mutually exclusive. For instance, in Figure 7.2 it would not be possible to combine any of the columns. Hence, where a variable has many different numerical values and it is sensible to group adjacent values together then a histogram is a worthwhile method of illustrating data.

A pie chart is a circle with segments highlighted to indicate proportionate sections of a total figure. For example, total company sales could be broken down into constituent parts. Sometimes you may wish to emphasize a particular segment by removing it a little way from the others. Pie charts are valuable for illustrating data where there are relatively few categories. Too many segments, especially where several represent a small proportion, can be confusing to the eye. Figure 7.3 shows how tourist types staying at a hotel can be illustrated in relation to their purpose of travel.

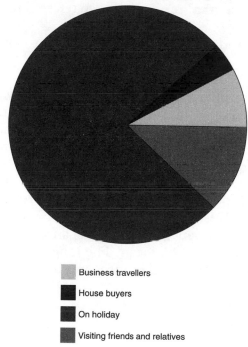

Business travellers

House buyers

On holiday

Visiting friends and relatives

**Figure 7.3** *Example of a pie chart*

## 7.3 Describing quantitative data

Illustrating the data by means of diagrams is not always sufficient to satisfy the aims and objectives of a quantitative survey. The numerical results of survey questions or variables are spread from the lowest value to the highest. This spread of data is referred to as a frequency distribution. For example, in a survey of tourists to a particular destination 400 respondents were asked, amongst other things, to state their age. It would be unwise to construct a frequency table of the results in a report as it would probably be very large and confusing. The information could be illustrated in a histogram, which would give some indication of the distribution of ages within the sample. However, it may be interesting to report what is the age of the youngest and oldest respondents and what is the average age within the sample. When further information of this kind is required there are a variety of descriptive statistical techniques which can be used. These techniques can be subdivided into two broad types:

1 **Measures of central tendency** (also referred to as measures of location)
2 **Measures of dispersion** (also referred to as measures of variation)

Measures of central tendency refer to values within a sample which are typical of all the values. One way of picturing this is to think of measures of central tendency which give the location of a value in the 'centre' of the sample data. The mean, median and mode (in decreasing order of importance) are three measures of central tendency which will be investigated in this chapter.

The second aspect, measures of dispersion, refer to how values are scattered, dispersed or spread within a sample. For example, what is the difference between the highest and lowest values or how many values lie close to the mean. The range, interquartile range, and standard deviation are three measures of dispersion which will be examined later in this chapter.

### Measures of central tendency

*Mean*

The most commonly used measure of central tendency is the mean. The definition of the mean is:

$$\text{Sample mean} = \frac{\text{Sum of observations}}{\text{Number of observations}}$$

As a formula the mean is represented as $\bar{x}$ (called x bar). The sum of observations is $\Sigma x$, where $\Sigma$ means the sum of and is represented by the Greek capital letter sigma and x is an observation or value in the sample. The number of observations in the sample is denoted as n. Thus the formula for the mean is:

$$\bar{x} = \frac{\Sigma x}{n}$$

For an example consider the following information.

| Destination | Number of 'Sunrest' Hotels located there |
|---|---|
| Belgium | 2 |
| France | 10 |
| Germany | 8 |
| Spain | 13 |
| Portugal | 7 |
| Italy | 7 |
| Greece | 9 |

By applying the formula for the mean to these data we find that

n = 7
$\Sigma x = 56$

and therefore

$$\bar{x} = \frac{56}{7}$$

= 8 hotels

This tells us that the mean number of Sunrest Hotels per country is 8. Whilst the mean is an accurate and useful measure of central tendency, you should remember that it can be affected by extreme values in a data set. In this example, it can be seen that the values for Germany, Greece, Portugal, France and Italy are close to the mean, while those for Belgium and Spain are not. The effect of extreme values on the mean is particularly pronounced where the data set contains very few values.

*Median*

The median of a sample of observations is the value of the middle item when the sample is arranged in rank order. Thus, for the same example, if the number of hotels in each country is placed in rank order, we find:

2, 7, 7, 8, 9, 10, 13

As the middle point of seven observations is the fourth, the median of this data set is 8.

Had there been an even number of observations in the data set, then the median would be the mid-point between the two middle values. The main disadvantage of the median is that equal weight is given to each observation in the data set regardless of its value.

*Mode*

The mode of a sample of observations is the value which occurs most often. Hence in the same data set the mode is 7 as it occurs more frequently than any other value. It should be remembered that a data set may have more than one mode. When a data set has one mode (as in this case), the distribution of values can be referred to as **unimodal**, whereas if two modes are present the distribution is said to be **bimodal**.

*Normal distribution*

If the mean, median and mode are calculated for a data set and found to be exactly the same value then the distribution is said to be **normal**. If the values for the data set are plotted on a graph then the results will be a smooth symmetrical bell shaped curve (see Figure 7.4).

If however, as in the data set used here where the mode was a value which was less than the median and mean, then the frequency curve plotted on a graph would have a **negative skew**. Similarly if the mode was a greater value than the median which in turn was greater than the mean, then the distribution would have **positive skew**. These types of distribution are shown in Figures 7.5 and 7.6.

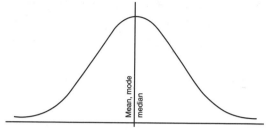

**Figure 7.4** *The frequency curve of a normal distribution*

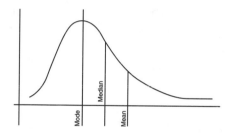

**Figure 7.5** *A frequency distribution with positive skew*

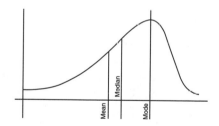

**Figure 7.6** *A frequency distribution with negative skew*

## Measures of dispersion

*The range*

The range of a data set is the difference between the highest and lowest values. For example, in a survey the age of each respondent is recorded in years, as follows:

34, 24, 27, 30, 40, 20, 41, 44, 45, 21, 36, 39

It can be seen that the oldest person is aged 45 and the youngest is 20. Hence the range is 25 years. Whist the range is a straightforward way of describing the scatter of values in a data set, it uses the extreme values and therefore the rest of the values are ignored.

### The interquartile range

As the name suggests, the interquartile range involves dividing a data set into quarters. After organizing the data set into rank order, the first quarter or quartile would come 25% from the beginning. This is called the **lower quartile**. The second quartile would come half way along the data set at the mid-point or median. The next quartile would come at the 75% mark and this is known as the **upper quartile**. The interquartile range is the difference between the upper quartile and the lower quartile, and is therefore concerned with the middle 50% of values within a data set. Hence for the same data set as used before, to find out the interquartile range we must first arrange the data set in rank order:

20, 21, 24, 27, 30, 34, 36, 39, 40, 41, 44, 45

From the previous section we can find the median, or middle number. As there are 12 values, the middle value falls between the 6th and the 7th, i.e. between 34 and 36, thus the median is 35. To work out the interquartile range we know that there will be three values in each quartile. The lower quartile will fall between the 3rd and the 4th value, i.e. between 24 and 27, the midpoint between these two values being 25.5. Similarly, the upper quartile, between the 9th and the 10th values, 40 and 41, is 40.5.

Thus in the example the interquartile range is

40.5 − 25.5 = 15

The value of the interquartile range is based on the fact that it avoids the influence of any extreme values in a data set, which could be confusing when the range is reported.

### Standard deviation

This measure investigates the spread of data in relation to the mean of the data set. Thus the standard deviation is calculated by determining the average distance of values from the mean. If the standard deviation is large, then this indicates that there is a greater variability in the data set. The formula for simple, numerical data is as follows:

$$Sd = \sqrt{\frac{\Sigma\,(x - \bar{x})^2}{n}}$$

Where  x = data
       $\bar{x}$ = mean
       n = number of values in the data set

**EXAMPLE**

A sample of ten tourists were asked to indicate how much they had spent on their lunch during a day trip. The amounts were rounded to the nearest pound, as follows:

   4, 6, 7, 7, 5, 8, 12, 15, 14, 12

To calculate the standard deviation (or sigma) you take the following steps.

1 First calculate the mean:

$$\frac{\Sigma x}{n} = \frac{90}{10} = £9$$

2 Now construct a table (see Table 7.3). From the table:
3 Find the deviations from the mean for each value of x.
4 Square the deviation from the mean for each value of x.
5 Total the squared deviations:
   i.e.     $\Sigma(x - \bar{x})^2$

**Table 7.3** *Calculating standard deviation*

| x | $(x - \bar{x})$ | $(x - \bar{x})^2$ |
|---|---|---|
| 4 | −5 | 25 |
| 6 | −3 | 9 |
| 7 | −2 | 4 |
| 7 | −2 | 4 |
| 5 | −4 | 16 |
| 8 | −1 | 1 |
| 12 | 3 | 9 |
| 15 | 6 | 36 |
| 14 | 5 | 25 |
| 12 | 3 | 9 |
| | $\Sigma(x - \bar{x})^2$ | 138 |

6 Now apply the formula, i.e.

$$= \sqrt{\frac{138}{10}}$$

$$= \sqrt{13.8}$$

$$= £3.71$$

When dealing with categorical data which is presented grouped, the formula for standard deviation is:

$$Sd = \sqrt{\frac{\Sigma f.x^2}{\Sigma f} - \left(\frac{\Sigma fx}{\Sigma f}\right)^2}$$

Where

f  = the frequency or number of items in a category
x  = the midpoint of a category

For example, a survey is carried out to find out how far tourists travelled to an historic building from their accommodation. The result for this question is as follows:

| Category | Number of respondents (frequency) |
|---|---|
| Under 10 miles | 5 |
| 10 but under 20 miles | 24 |
| 20 but under 30 miles | 35 |
| 30 but under 40 miles | 31 |
| 40 but under 50 miles | 23 |
| 50 but under 70 miles | 8 |
| 70 but under 100 miles | 5 |
| 100 but under 150 miles | 3 |
| 150 miles or more | 1 |

Notice the categories are not all equal in size. Now construct a table (see Table 7.4) and then apply the formula.

**Table 7.4** *Calculating standard deviation for categorical data*

| Class | Midpoint x | Frequency f | fx | f.x² |
|---|---|---|---|---|
| Under 10 miles | 5 | 5 | 25 | 125 |
| 10 but under 20 miles | 15 | 24 | 360 | 5400 |
| 20 but under 30 miles | 25 | 35 | 875 | 21875 |
| 30 but under 40 miles | 35 | 31 | 1085 | 37975 |
| 40 but under 50 miles | 45 | 23 | 1035 | 46575 |
| 50 but under 70 miles | 60 | 8 | 480 | 28800 |
| 70 but under 100 miles | 85 | 5 | 425 | 36125 |
| 100 but under 150 miles | 125 | 3 | 375 | 46875 |
| 150 miles or more* | 175 | 1 | 175 | 30625 |
| (*Upper limit assumed to be 200) | | | | |
| Σ | | 135 | 4835 | 254375 |

$$Sd = \sqrt{\frac{254375}{135} - \left(\frac{4835}{135}\right)^2}$$

$$= \sqrt{1884.3 - (35.8)^2}$$

$$= \sqrt{1884.3 - 1281.6}$$

$$= \sqrt{602.7}$$

$$= 24.6 \text{ miles}$$

## 7.4 Analysing quantitative data

### Overview

In the previous section we referred to the expression 'normal distribution' where the mean, median and mode of a data set occupied the same value. If the distribution for a data set is normal, then the laws of probability are such that:

- about 68% of all observations will fall between the mean and 1 standard deviation
- about 95% of all observations will fall between the mean and 2 standard deviations
- about 99% of all observations will fall between the mean and 3 standard deviations

You may be wondering what in real life is a normal distribution and how would you know if your data set was one. When very large surveys are undertaken of the general public, variables such as age, height, weight, etc. are considered to be normally distributed, thus over 99% of all answers or observations will fall within 3 standard deviations of the mean. If you can assume that your data set are normally distributed (for example instructing the computer to graphically represent the distribution and noting that it is a smooth symmetrical bell-shape), then this has an implication for the nature of analytical statistical techniques you can perform on the data. When it comes to analytical techniques, there is a broad twofold distinction:

- **Parametric statistics:** This assumes that the sample data set has a normal distribution. Often these tests will use the mean and standard deviation and involve cardinal (numerical) data.
- **Non-parametric statistics:** These tests do not assume that the data set approximates a normal distribution and are therefore more common in the analysis of market research information. Often the data can be in the form of categories or ranks.

### Hypothesis testing

In the statistical analysis of market research information we are often concerned with comparing whether a particular variable, such as income, for example, has any influence on another variable, such as type of holiday purchased. When results of a statistical test to determine the influence of a variable in this way are produced, we are often required to indicate whether the differences found are sufficiently large to state that, say, income level has a significant bearing on holiday type. Before learning how to undertake such a statistical test it is important to express the question which lies behind the analysis in the correct way.

Statisticians do this by stating what is called a **hypothesis**. It is convention to be cautious when writing statements and therefore it is normal at the beginning of any statistical test to state what is termed the **null hypothesis**. This assumes that there is no difference, association or relationship between the two variables or samples in the analysis. Thus, before investigating the effect of income on holiday type, we would start by expressing a null hypothesis, namely:

There is no significant relationship/difference/association between a respondent's income and the type of holiday which is chosen.

This gives the researcher a context with which to apply the test, after which the null hypothesis can be accepted or rejected.

## Levels of significance

If we are in a position to reject a null hypothesis, we are indicating that there are significant differences between the two variables or samples we are testing. The immediate question which follows this is 'how big does the difference have to be before it becomes significant?' In a sense deciding on a 'cut-off' point may seem rather arbitrary, like asking 'how far does a tourist have to travel to say they have been "far away"?' In statistical analysis there are, conventionally, two cut-off points. These are the 5% level and the 1% level (often referred to as the 0.05 level and the 0.01 level).

What this means is that at the 0.05 level we are indicating that we are 95% confident that there is a significant difference and there is a 5% probability that the result has occurred by random chance. Consequently, the 0.01 level is more stringent. Here we are 99% confident of a significant difference and there is a 1% probability that the result has occurred by chance.

When carrying out statistical tests to measure the difference between two variables or samples, it is important to decide at what level to accept or reject a null hypothesis. Sometimes a difference that is significant at the 0.05 level is said to be 'significant', while at the 0.01 level 'highly significant'. Such words may add very little to the actual figures but may make the researcher feel more confident in reporting the results.

In carrying out analytical statistics it should be remembered that:

1  the tests should have been previously specified and must relate to the objectives of the research;
2  a null hypothesis is written prior to each test;
3  an appropriate level of significance is determined prior to each test.

It is now possible to review some of the commonly used statistical methods in the analysis of survey data.

## Two useful tests

Two tests have been selected for illustrative purposes here. These are:

- The chi-square test
- Spearman's rank correlation

These tests are both non-parametric, thus assumptions about the data set relating to a normal distribution are not necessary. These tests are also very relevant to the analysis of questions from survey data. While statistical computer software packages can easily perform these tests, to undertake them with a calculator is feasible and should not be ruled out for small samples.

### Chi-square test

This is one of the most widely used tests in social science statistics. The chi-square test (or chi-squared test) is denoted by the Greek letter $\chi$ chi (pronounced 'ky' as in 'sky') and is used to test the level of significance in the association or relationship between the answers given to one question (usually an independent variable) and the answers given to another question (a dependent variable). To illustrate how chi-square works it will be useful to follow an example.

In a survey the following results were found.

**Question 30**
*Sex of respondent*

|  | Frequency |
|---|---|
| Male | 90 |
| Female | 110 |

**Question 22**
*How would you rate the sports facilities of the hotel?*

| Rating | Frequency |
|---|---|
| Excellent | 35 |
| Good | 40 |
| Average | 45 |
| Poor | 50 |
| Very poor | 30 |

Next it is common to **cross-tabulate** the answers to the two questions. What this involves is showing how many males and females gave each of the ratings scores to Question 22. The result of this is shown in Table 7.5.

**Table 7.5** *Cross-tabulation of sex by rating of sports facilities*

| Rating | Sex of respondent | | Row total |
|---|---|---|---|
|  | Male | Female |  |
| Excellent | 23 | 12 | 35 |
| Good | 27 | 13 | 40 |
| Average | 20 | 25 | 45 |
| Poor | 12 | 38 | 50 |
| Very poor | 8 | 22 | 30 |
| Column total | 90 | 110 | 200 |

Table 7.5 shows that of the 35 people who rated the sports facilities as excellent, 23 were male and 12 were female. Similarly,

of the 30 respondents who rated the facilities as very poor, 22 were female and 8 were male. The cross-tabulation table itself gives some indication of a relationship in that it appears that males rate the facilities more highly than females. However, there are more females than males, so is there a significant relationship? This is where the chi-square test is valuable, and is carried out in several stages.

### Stage 1  An assertion is made

From the frequency table and cross-tabulation results it appears that the sex of the respondent (the independent variable in this case) may have an influence on the rating of the sports facilities in the hotel (the dependent variable).

### Stage 2  The assertion is converted into the form of a null hypothesis and the required level of significance determined

The null hypothesis for this example would be:

There is no association between the sex of the respondent and the rating of the sports facilities.

The 0.01 level is determined as suitable for this test, being sufficiently stringent to be confident.

### Stage 3  The information is arranged in the form of a cross-tabulation table and the column and row totals noted

See Table 7.5.

### Stage 4  The frequencies expected by chance are calculated for each cell of the table

This assumes what the frequency for each cell would be if there was no association between the two questions, i.e. they were independent of each other. One way of picturing this is to imagine you were comparing a male/female question against a yes/no question. You interviewed 100 people, of which 50 were male and 50 were female, 50 said yes and 50 said no. The expected value in each cell would be 25, as shown below:

| Expected value | Male | Female | Row total |
|---|---|---|---|
| Yes | 25 | 25 | 50 |
| No | 25 | 25 | 50 |
| Column total | 50 | 50 | 100 |

The expected values are evenly split in each cell because the row and column totals are the same value. If there are different values for the column and row totals, then to work out the expected value for a specific cell you must multiply that cell's row total by its column total and divide by the grand total (that is the total number of people interviewed or sample size). Thus:

$$\text{Expected value} = \frac{\text{Row total} \times \text{Column total}}{\text{Grand total}}$$

In the example already begun, the result of finding the expected values can be expressed in a new cross-tabulation table, as shown in Table 7.6.

## Stage 5 Apply the chi-square test using the formula

$$\chi^2 = \Sigma \frac{(O - E)^2}{E}$$

Where
O = the observed value
E = the expected value

To do this we must work through another table, as shown in Table 7.7.

**Table 7.6** *Cross-tabulation of sex by rating of sports facilities with observed and expected values*

| Observed value<br>Expected value | Sex of respondent | | Row total |
|---|---|---|---|
| Rating | Male | Female | |
| Excellent | 23<br>15.8 | 12<br>19.3 | 35 |
| Good | 27<br>18 | 13<br>22 | 40 |
| Average | 20<br>20.3 | 25<br>24.8 | 45 |
| Poor | 12<br>22.5 | 38<br>27.5 | 50 |
| Very poor | 8<br>13.5 | 12<br>16.5 | 30 |
| Column total | 90 | 110 | 200 |

**Table 7.7** *Calculating chi-square*

| Observed<br>values | Expected<br>values | | | |
|---|---|---|---|---|
| O | E | O – E | $(O - E)^2$ | $(O - E)^2 \div E$ |
| 23 | 15.8 | 7.2 | 51.8 | 3.6 |
| 12 | 19.3 | −7.3 | 53.3 | 2.8 |
| 27 | 18 | 9 | 81 | 4.5 |
| 13 | 22 | −9 | 81 | 3.7 |
| 20 | 20.3 | −0.3 | 0.5 | 0.0 |
| 25 | 24.8 | 0.2 | 0.0 | 0.0 |
| 12 | 22.5 | −10.5 | 110.3 | 4.9 |
| 38 | 27.5 | 10.5 | 110.3 | 4.0 |
| 8 | 13.5 | −5.5 | 30.3 | 2.2 |
| 12 | 16.5 | −4.5 | 20.3 | 1.2 |
| | | | $\Sigma$ | 26.9 |

Thus the chi-square test statistic is 26.9.

## Stage 6 Calculate the degrees of freedom

The degrees of freedom give some meaning to the test statistic. In this case it relates the number of items in the sample upon which the test was based. In this example there were 5 rows and 2 columns. The degrees of freedom are given by:

$$df = (r - 1) \times (c - 1)$$

where

$r$ = the number of rows
$c$ = the number of columns

In this example

$$df = (5 - 1) \times (2 - 1)$$
$$= 4 \times 1$$
$$= 4$$

## Stage 7 At the appropriate level of significance and degrees of freedom the result is read from a table of chi-square distribution

Tables of the chi-square distribution are available in many statistical text books (see Slater and Ascroft, 1990, for a full set). A shortened version is shown in Table 7.8.

## Stage 8 The null hypothesis is either accepted or rejected depending on the required level of significance

In this example the chi-square test statistic of 26.9 is greater than the value in the table (13.3) therefore we can reject the null hypothesis. Thus we are 99.9% confident that there is some association between the sex of the respondent and the rating of sports facilities, and acknowledge that there is a 0.1% probability that this result has occurred by chance. If the chi-square value had been less than the value in the table for the given significance level and degrees of freedom, we would have accepted the null hypothesis.

**Table 7.8** *Percentage points of the chi-square distribution*

| Probability level | | 0.05 | 0.01 |
|---|---|---|---|
| Degrees of freedom | 1 | 3.84 | 6.63 |
| | 2 | 5.99 | 9.21 |
| | 3 | 7.81 | 11.3 |
| | 4 | 9.49 | 13.3 |
| | 5 | 11.1 | 15.1 |
| | 6 | 12.6 | 16.8 |
| | 7 | 14.1 | 18.5 |
| | 8 | 15.5 | 20.3 |
| | 9 | 16.9 | 21.7 |
| | 10 | 18.3 | 23.2 |
| | 12 | 21.0 | 26.2 |
| | 14 | 23.7 | 29.1 |
| | 16 | 26.3 | 32.0 |
| | 18 | 28.9 | 34.8 |
| | 20 | 31.4 | 37.6 |

In this example the table value for 4 degrees of freedom is 9.49 at the 0.05 level and 13.3 at the 0.01 level (the level of significance determined for the example in stage 2).

## Stage 9  An inference is made from the result

Having rejected the null hypothesis we are now indicating that there is an association between the sex of the respondent and their rating of the sports facilities but the chi-square test does not tell us what the association is. This we must infer. The easiest way to do this is to return to the table where the observed values in the survey were set against the expected values if no association was apparent (Table 7.6) and not where there are large differences in the cells. Here we see that more than expected males rated the facilities as excellent or good, and fewer than expected females gave these ratings. Conversely, fewer than expected males rated the facilities as poor or very poor, whereas as more females than expected gave these ratings. Thus we can infer that males are more likely to rate the sports facilities highly and females are more likely to give lower ratings for the sports facilities in the hotel. The job of evaluating these results and changing the facilities to be more attractive to females may well be the outcome of this investigation.

## OTHER POINTS TO REMEMBER WITH CHI-SQUARE

Whilst chi-square is a valuable and useful analytical technique in market research, there are some conditions which affect its validity. The principal problem with chi-square is where the cross-tabulation has a large number of rows and columns but the sample size is small. When this happens there may be many cells which are empty or have very low observed values and expected frequencies. This can severely weaken the test. As a general rule you should not use the chi-square test if more than 20% of the cells have expected frequencies of less than 5 and if any of the cells have an expected frequency of less than 1 (Norusis, 1990). If this is the case you should consider combining categories together to reduce the size of the cross-tabulation table, but only if there is a rationale for doing so. For example, excellent and good could be combined as could poor and very poor, reducing the rows from 5 to 3. However, putting together males and females into one category would defeat the object of the test and be without logic.

On this latter point, it can be seen that sample size influences whether a test such as chi-square is suitable or not. Where you anticipate using chi-square, the requirements of the test may help you to judge the overall sample size of a survey in the planning stages (see Chapter 4).

### Spearman's rank correlation coefficient

This test is used to describe the relationship in ordinal (ranked) characteristics. This can be useful where it is difficult to measure a particular characteristic and ranking the data can overcome the problem. For example, a tour operator sells eight different holiday programmes (family holidays, young adult, retired, winter sports, etc.). These holidays are sold in the UK and Germany, as shown in Table 7.9.

**Table 7.9** *Sales of different holidays in UK and Germany*

| Holiday type | UK (£) (000) | Germany (DM) (000000) |
|:---:|:---:|:---:|
| 1 | 15,004 | 38,424 |
| 2 | 22,483 | 25,500 |
| 3 | 7,896 | 12,986 |
| 4 | 14,283 | 44,824 |
| 5 | 78,975 | 93,611 |
| 6 | 3,242 | 3,100 |
| 7 | 28,227 | 13,819 |
| 8 | 4,591 | 2,986 |

Because of exchange rates changing over a season, together with the different size of each market, it is difficult to compare the relative value of the information. However, to compare the popularity of each holiday type in the two countries one way of simplifying the information would be to rank it, as shown in Table 7.10.

**Table 7.10** *Rankings of holidays sold in UK and Germany by holiday type*

| Holiday type | Rank in UK | Rank in Germany |
|:---:|:---:|:---:|
| 1 | 4 | 3 |
| 2 | 3 | 4 |
| 3 | 6 | 6 |
| 4 | 5 | 2 |
| 5 | 1 | 1 |
| 6 | 8 | 7 |
| 7 | 2 | 5 |
| 8 | 7 | 8 |

Here the holiday types have been ranked by the value in each country. To test whether there is a statistical association between the sets of rankings we can apply the Spearman's rank correlation coefficient, explained in the following stages.

## Stage 1  Determine a null hypothesis and the significance level

Null hypothesis: There is no association between the rankings of the holidays sold in the UK and Germany.

This is to be tested at the 0.05 level.

## Stage 2  Calculate the differences between the ranks, square them and sum the total

**Table 7.11** *Calculating the differences in the rankings*

| Holiday type | Rank in UK | Rank in Germany | Difference (d) | $d^2$ |
|:---:|:---:|:---:|:---:|:---:|
| 1 | 4 | 3 | 1 | 1 |
| 2 | 3 | 4 | −1 | 1 |
| 3 | 6 | 6 | 0 | 0 |
| 4 | 5 | 2 | 3 | 9 |
| 5 | 1 | 1 | 0 | 0 |
| 6 | 8 | 7 | 1 | 1 |
| 7 | 2 | 5 | −3 | 9 |
| 8 | 7 | 8 | −1 | 1 |
| | | | $\Sigma$ | 22 |

## Stage 3  Apply the formula

The formula for Spearman's rank correlation coefficient ($r_s$) is:

$$r_s = 1 - [6\Sigma d^2 / n(n^2 - 1)]$$

Where n = the number of ranks. In our example this gives:

$$
\begin{aligned}
r_s &= 1 - 6 \times 22/8(8^2 - 1) \\
&= 1 - 132/8 \times 63 \\
&= 1 - 132/504 \\
&= 1 - 0.26 \\
r_s &= 0.74
\end{aligned}
$$

The formula will always produce a figure for $r_s$ which lies between +1 and −1. If the value of $r_s$ is very close to +1 then the two countries will have similar ranks (be positively correlated), and if the value of $r_s$ is −1 they will have opposite ranks (negative correlation). A value of 0 represents no statistical correlation. However, as in this case, achieving extreme values is quite rare. As a general rule, if the value of $r_s$ lies between −0.5 and +0.5 you can accept the null hypothesis and indicate that there is no statistical association (unless you have in excess of 15 ranks). Values greater or less than this may indicate some degree of statistical significance and tables are again needed to determine acceptance or rejection of the null hypothesis.

### Stage 4 The test statistic is compared against probability tables for Spearman's rank correlation coefficient

Appropriate tables are shown in Table 7.12.

**Table 7.12** *Spearman's rank correlation coefficient probability tables (where n = number ranks)*

| | Probability values (one sided) | |
| n | 0.05 | 0.01 |
|---|---|---|
| 4 | 1.000 | – |
| 5 | 0.900 | 1.000 |
| 6 | 0.829 | 0.943 |
| 7 | 0.714 | 0.893 |
| 8 | 0.643 | 0.833 |
| 9 | 0.600 | 0.783 |
| 10 | 0.564 | 0.746 |
| 12 | 0.504 | 0.701 |
| 14 | 0.456 | 0.645 |
| 16 | 0.425 | 0.601 |
| 18 | 0.399 | 0.564 |
| 20 | 0.377 | 0.534 |
| 22 | 0.359 | 0.508 |
| 24 | 0.343 | 0.485 |
| 26 | 0.329 | 0.465 |
| 28 | 0.317 | 0.448 |
| 30 | 0.306 | 0.432 |

Hence we see that at the 0.05 level, with 8 ranks a test statistic of 0.74 exceeds the table value of 0.643.

**Stage 5 The null hypothesis is accepted or rejected and an inference is made from the result.**

At the 0.05 level we can reject the null hypothesis and indicate that the rankings for the UK and Germany are associated. The inference from this would be that the popular holiday products sold in the UK are similarly popular in Germany. Note, however, that had a higher significance level been set this would not be the case, as the data show that there are some differences.

## 7.5 Analysing qualitative data

### Introduction

Unlike quantitative analysis, where there are tried and tested techniques, qualitative methods of analysis are not so clear cut. It is not possible to state that under certain circumstances the 'such and such' test should be used. This may well leave the first-time researcher unsure of whether their attempts to categorize transcriptions of interviews are appropriate, as finding a yardstick to test them against is so difficult. The purpose of the qualitative research is instrumental in determining how it should be analysed. Qualitative research, as mentioned in Chapter 2, is sometimes used to explore a particular topic and inform the design of a quantitative inquiry. In these circumstances detailed notes which the researcher makes from the experience of conducting lengthy interviews and focus groups may be sufficient to help in the construction of a structured questionnaire for pilot testing. However, as was stressed in Chapter 2, to consider qualitative research as being solely for this exploratory function is to miss the point and value of this approach. Increasingly the use of focus groups, panels, longitudinal studies and in-depth interviews are becoming more and more common in market research. The case studies of Chapter 2 demonstrated some examples of where qualitative research was the chosen approach. Where this is the case, though, how should the results of interviews and the like be analysed?

Unfortunately, as indicated, qualitative methods of analysis are inconspicuous when compared to quantitative techniques. However, one method, called 'framework', provides a useful example to demonstrate the basics of qualitative analysis. It should be remembered that any analysis must be directed to the aims and objectives of the research. While this may seem an obvious and unnecessary statement, a particular feature of qualitative data is the huge amount of paper, words, recordings, etc., which enable the researcher to become easily side-tracked.

## The 'framework' method

The method of qualitative analysis which will be explained in this section was initially developed by SCPR (Social and Community Planning Research) as reported by Ritchie and Spencer (1994). Qualitative methods of analysis change in relation to the data to which they are applied. As such the framework method is a generic method, providing a versatile means for qualitative analysis, rather than being a highly specific technique. It provides a procedural structure to which the researcher can apply his/her own data. As such it can be applied to a wide variety of qualitative methods of data collection with differing aims and objectives.

It should be remembered that often qualitative studies are concerned with exploring and investigating deeply a particular phenomenon. Thus, when analysing qualitative data the approach taken should be complementary to this. The data from qualitative studies are often in the form of transcripts of tape recorded interviews with individuals and groups. Typically it may take several hours before the researcher has transcribed and feels fully aware of the content of a short interview with a single respondent. The process of transcribing a recording often gives the researcher certain 'hunches' in how aspects of the data relate to the research questions posed. The benefit of a method such as the framework is that it allows the mass of data and hunches from the transcripts to be organized in a structured way. Essentially, the framework method involves five key stages:

1 Familiarization
2 Identifying a thematic framework
3 Indexing
4 Charting
5 Mapping and interpretation

Each of these will now be briefly examined in turn. For a more detailed explanation, the reader should refer to Ritchie and Spencer (1994).

### FRAMEWORK STAGE 1 FAMILIARIZATION

This involves the researcher who is to perform the analysis, becoming familiar with the scope, nature and richness of the data. This is particularly important where staff other than the analyst have undertaken the interviews, led focus groups or transcribed the recordings. Thus the analyst must gain an overview to conceptualize the material and put his/her hunches into context. During this stage the analyst makes notes on themes coming from the data which relate to the aims and objectives of the research.

### FRAMEWORK STAGE 2 IDENTIFYING A THEMATIC FRAMEWORK

This stage requires the further development of the notes from the familiarization becoming organized into recurring themes. Again reference to the original aims and objectives is crucial. Eventually the data are sorted into a framework of themes which relate to the research questions of the study. This stage remains fairly descriptive in character in the sense that it represents a stage beyond initial sifting but only as far as the identification of general themes. However, within this stage the thematic framework which is developed can be tested for its suitability against several transcripts. Often there will be discrepancies or anomalies where the themes identified do not hold up against the actual data. It is likely that several attempts of 'toing and froing' between a framework of themes and its applicability to the data will take place. Once a suitable thematic framework has been developed the next stage flows naturally.

### FRAMEWORK STAGE 3 INDEXING

This stage relates to the thematic framework being applied to the whole data in a systematic way. Thus specific comments and phrases made by the respondents can be 'indexed' within the thematic framework. Depending upon the nature of the data collection and the form of the data, the indexes may be numbers, symbols or annotations on the margins of the transcripts. Index cards which are colour coded may also be useful. Inevitably as this stage is applied to the whole data set, there will be instances where the researcher must apply a certain degree of judgement over how particular statements are coded within the indexing system. To improve accuracy, Ritchie and Spencer (1994) recommend that the researcher tries out their indexing system on colleagues to allow judgements and assumptions to be evaluated.

## FRAMEWORK STAGE 4   CHARTING

Following the indexing of statements and phrases, it is now possible to develop a more complete assessment of the data. To represent the extent of the material, charting can be undertaken. This involves the removal of the key phrases which were indexed in the transcripts and placing them in a table, matrix or chart in relation to a particular theme. The precise nature of the chart will relate to the nature of the data, the research questions posed and the thematic framework defined by the analyst. Typically a chart will have a research question as a column heading and each case (or respondent) as a row of the table. Within each cell the themes identified can be located together with the phrase or statement which was indexed from the transcript. It is recommended that when reporting data in this way the same chart layout is used for each research question to ease comparisons between the chart.

An example of this process was applied to a study of local resident attitudes to tourism in a small seaside resort. Twelve respondents were selected for interview using a stratified sampling system suggested by Krippendorf (1987). One of the many research questions posed was what impact tourism had on employment opportunities generally, and specifically in relation to female opportunities. Scrutiny of the transcripts of the in-depth interviews of this latter aspect resulted in a threefold division among the respondents. Thus after testing, there were three themes identified in respect of how tourism had affected female employment opportunities. These were 'gender irrelevant', indicating little differences in male and female employment as a result of tourism, 'female favoured' suggesting more employment opportunities for females and 'structural change' suggesting a more general change in the structure of employment as a result of tourism. From the transcripts key phrases made by the respondents were 'indexed' under each of these themes. The results of this process could then be charted as shown in Table 7.13.

**Table 7.13** *An example of charted qualitative data*

| Respondent | Research question<br>*What effects has tourism had on female employment opportunities?* |
| --- | --- |
| A | Female favoured<br>*On balance I think there are more jobs for women* |
| B | Gender irrelevant<br>*Most jobs are for both male and female* |
| C | Gender irrelevant<br>*They can be done by men and women* |
| E | Gender irrelevant<br>*Casual labour can apply quite equally to men or women* |
| F | Structural change<br>*Cleaning jobs have mushroomed* |
| G | Female favoured<br>*A lot of the new boutiques which opened are owned by women* |
| H | Gender irrelevant<br>*I don't think there are any differences* |
| I | Structural change<br>*There's a lot more jobs anyway in the summer now* |
| J | Gender irrelevant<br>*Both men and women are unemployed round here anyway* |
| K | Female favoured<br>*There's more jobs for women in the tourist trade* |
| L | Female favoured<br>*A greater percentage of women can work in tourism* |

## FRAMEWORK STAGE 5 MAPPING AND INTERPRETATION

The charting process of the previous stage is a means to facilitate the mapping and interpretation of the data as a whole. The final stage of the framework method is the most difficult, and is the most creative. It involves the evaluation and discussion of the data in relation to the original aims and objectives of the study. Ritchie and Spencer (1994) suggest that six features of qualitative research are often what the analyst returns to at this stage, namely:

1  defining concepts;
2  mapping range and nature of phenomena;
3  creating typologies;
4  finding associations;
5  providing explanations;
6  developing strategies.

The emphasis on each of these is guided by the study aims. What is involved is comparing charts, looking for patterns and connections, seeking instances where respondents complement or contradict each other and searching for explanations to the research questions. For the research to be useful, the researcher must evaluate the data and draw out conclusions rather than simply reporting how many cases supported a particular theme. This stage requires reflection, intuition and imagination on the part of the analyst. If the framework process has worked, then it should be possible for the analyst to visualize the results, judge their importance and provide an appropriate interpretation.

## Judging qualitative research

The framework method is only one method of analysing qualitative data. However, its inclusion here is becuase it is flexible and versatile in application. It provides a logical sequence to approaching the mass of qualitative material and helps to keep the analyst on a pathway which will keep the original purpose of the research in mind.

As qualitative research is open to the judgement of the researcher, it is often difficult to critically evaluate its worth. Moreover, in many instances considerable attention is given to the interpretation of the results rather than the methods devised by the researcher to achieve this analysis. Strauss and Corbin (1990) suggest that when evaluating qualitative research sufficient attention should be given to the 'validity, reliability and credibility of the data ... the adequacy of the research process ... (and the) ... judgements made about the empirical grounding of the research findings'. Of particular importance then in the judgement of qualitative research is the reporting of the whole research method to demonstrate rigour and logic in the process.

# Summary

This chapter has attempted to convey some principal issues which the researcher faces when dealing with the data. Some of the statistical vocabulary has been presented and the need for careful prior planning has been stressed. It was not intended that this chapter should be a shortened statistical text, as that is better dealt with elsewhere and requires formal training. However, the information provided should enable you to be more informed and be more critical of data presented to you.

# Exercises

1 Outline the differences between categorical, ordinal and cardinal data. Give examples of each form.
2 Explain what is meant by the following terms: variable, value, case, independent and dependent variable.
3 When using a frequency table, assess when it would be more appropriate to use the valid percentage or cumulative percentage to explain a result.
4 Determine when it is more appropriate to use a histogram rather than a bar chart.
5 Define the terms mean, median and mode.
6 Discuss the principal difference in the assumptions of parametric statistics and non-parametric statistics.
7 Explain the five stages of the framework method of qualitative data analysis.

# Further reading

### Quantitative Analysis

Fink, A. (1995). *How to analyze survey data*. London: Sage Publications.

This is the eighth part of a nine-volume survey kit. It is divided into three main parts. Part One investigates data types and descriptive statistics, Part Two examines relationships and correlations and the third part looks at some commonly used statistical methods for surveys. For the tourism student the book is useful and the explanations are clear; however, examples are often given from a medical perspective.

Norusis, M.J. (1990). *The SPSS Guide to Data Analysis*. Chicago: SPSS Inc.

This book relates to the SPSS software for statistical analysis which is commonly taught on degree courses and is widely used by market research organizations as well as for academic research. The explanations of statistical techniques are extensive and go into instructions for performing the tests using the software on computer.

Slater, R. and Ascroft, P. (1990). *Quantitative techniques in a business context*. London: Chapman and Hall.

This book introduces statistical techniques essentially for students on business studies courses. There are extensive examples given from a general business background. The chapters on illustrating data, describing data and marketing and market research are particularly useful in the context here.

## Qualitative analysis

Bryman, A. and Burgess, R.G. (eds) (1994). *Analyzing Qualitative Data*. London: Routledge.

This book has twelve chapters covering a wide variety of aspects relating to qualitative research. Of particular use are the chapters linking qualitative and quantitative data analysis (by Mason) and on qualitative data analysis by Ritchie and Spencer.

Strauss, A. and Corbin, J. (1990). *Basics of qualitative research*. London: Sage Publications.

This book provides a useful background to approaching qualitative analysis. It is divided into three parts: basic considerations, coding procedures and adjunctive procedures (including writing up and diagrams). Some of the aspects regarding sampling given little attention in many texts are explained in some detail in this source.

Psathas, G. (1995). *Conversation analysis: The study of talk-in-inter-action*. London: Sage Publications.

This book presents how to properly undertake the analysis of qualitative interviews. The book develops a conceptual framework for conversation analysis and demonstrates transcription techniques and analytical procedures.

Morse, J.M. (ed.) (1994). *Critical issues in qualitative research methods*. London: Sage Publications.

This extensive book has 18 chapters covering different aspects of qualitative research. These include critiques of the use of focus groups, video, secondary data and interviews. There are also chapters on analysing data and writing up projects. This book is not intended as a primer for those who have yet to undertake qualitative research, but is useful for those who are interested in improving their research or have a general interest in the approach.

*Writing up and presenting the results*

## Learning objectives

- To appreciate the different approaches to writing and presenting findings in relation to the type of research carried out.
- To understand how to organize the main sections of research reports.
- To learn how to prepare and arrange presentations.

## 8.1 Introduction

As mentioned in Chapter 3, the final stage of the research process is the communication of the findings. Normally this will involve a written report and may also include giving a presentation. The format for the report or presentation will, to a certain extent, be dictated by the type of research undertaken.

In academic research, reports of the findings of research projects are often published as papers in journals such as *Tourism Management* or *Annals of Tourism Research*. Here the format of the paper is often prescribed by the 'house style' of the journal. Aspects such as the illustrations, method of referencing as well as the length of the text must fit with the journal's own criteria. Moreover, before publication may proceed the paper is 'refereed' by other academics who may sit on an editorial board for the journal. Referees may recommend rejecting the publication or suggest amendments before the paper is accepted. Academics may, alternatively, report their findings in books either as a whole text or as a chapter in an edited text. Here, again, there may be certain requirements of format made by the publisher or editor. Often academics will aim to present a paper at a conference where they can speak about their research findings to others interested in the subject. Most conferences issue the 'proceedings' of a conference which represent a written form of the academics' speech.

A form where students report their findings is in support of a particular qualification. These can range from a special study or major project for a Higher National Diploma, through an honours project or dissertation for a first degree to the thesis for a masters' or doctorate qualification. Here too, the awarding body may require certain features to be included in the format of any written material. Additionally, the qualification may involve an oral presentation or examination.

With applied or action research where, typically, projects are undertaken on behalf of an employer, the results are often communicated in both written and verbal form. Reports of research may be read by senior management, councillors, or shareholders depending on the nature of the employer. In this case an executive summary, which is a shortened version of the principal findings, is usually required. This is because busy executives or councillors can get a 'flavour' of the report and decide how much of the rest of the report they need to (or are willing to) read. In addition, employee researchers will often be asked to give a presentation of their work to a meeting of senior colleagues.

Where the nature of the research has been a consultancy project a similar pattern is usually found. The format for the results in terms of written report and any presentation will have been specified in the contract. Additionally, the consultant may be required to submit written interim reports and give presentations at client meetings.

It can be seen that whatever the type of research, and while there may be certain guidelines or constraints in terms of format, the reporting and presentation of the project are crucial to the researcher. To academics future funding opportunities, reputation and promotion prospects are, in part, determined by the success of the publication of their research. To the HND, degree, MA/MSc or PhD student, a significant part of passing their examination is down to skill in writing up their findings and defending them orally. To the employee researcher their opportunities to get future interesting projects, promotion prospects and company performance may to a certain degree be directly related to completing and reporting his/her research. Finally, to the consultant their chance of future contracts and financial survival are directly related to their performance and ability to communicate effectively. Hence, it would seem that if any researcher is to be truly successful, and achieve job satisfaction, writing up and presenting results must be done well!

When embarking on the writing up process, it is necessary to first consider the readership. This can influence the type of language and emphasis given to particular sections. The consultancy report may have a greater focus on the findings and give more specific recommendations than would an academic paper. In the latter case, the academic may need to give greater depth to the methods of data collection, sampling techniques and types of analysis than would a consultant's report.

Writing up and giving presentations are not easy but can be very rewarding. Unfortunately, however, they are often left until the very end of a project when time pressures for completion are greatest. Too often data collection and analysis overrun and eat into the time allowed for writing up. While, for some, the deadline looming helps to focus the mind and motivate the writer, it is probably safer to recognize the difficulty and plan ahead. Some sections of a report could be written as a first draft while the data collection is underway. The aims and objectives, introduction, methodology, bibliography and some appendices could be prepared in advance before the researcher becomes too involved in the data analysis. The aim of this chapter is to help in this process. It is divided into two parts to give some practical guidelines for preparing a report or planning a presentation.

## 8.2  Writing reports

### Sequence

As previously mentioned, the type of the research approach, readership and place of publication will influence the nature of a report. However, commonly, most reports will include a variation of the following:

Title
Preface or Foreword (or both)
Acknowledgements
Contents page

List of tables
List of figures
Summary or Abstract
Introduction
Aims and objectives
Methods
Results
Discussion
Recommendations
Conclusion
References or Bibliography (or both)
Appendices

Each of these will now be examined in turn.

### Title

On the front cover of a report will be the title of the work, the name of the author, the year in which it was completed and the name of the employer (action research) or client (consultancy). The title should reflect the purpose of the study and be as concise as possible. Occasionally, as is more common in books, the first page will also be a title page. This repeats similar information but may also include the details of the publisher.

### Preface or Foreword

Again these are more common in books than reports but are mentioned here for completeness. A foreword is normally written by a series editor or eminent individual in the subject area. It is an introduction in support of the book covering its purpose and scope. A preface is usually written by the author and typically outlines the principal themes to be covered, the general approach, intended readership and other similar points.

### Acknowledgements

This is an expression of gratitude to those who have helped the author in the research. As such they are common to both books and reports. It is usual in reports to acknowledge the help of the sponsors of the research, staff who collected the data, the respondents of a survey and any others who provided technical assistance. Where permission from another author or organization was sought to include some of their work in the text (especially when the report is published), this is also acknowledged.

### Contents page

This reports the page numbers of each major section.

### Lists of tables and figures

Where tables or figures have been included in the main body of the report they are titled and listed following the contents. Sometimes tables and figures are numbered consecutively throughout the text (from 1, 2 to 40, etc.) or by each section (4.1, 7.2, meaning the first table or figure in Section 4 and the second table in Section 7). The page number is supplied by each entry.

### Summary or Abstract

A summary is of the whole report providing the reader with a shortened version of the aims and objectives, methods, results, recommendations and conclusions. Only the most important findings are included which allow executives (in the case of an executive summary) to be aware of any recommendations prior to reading the main text.

For research reports which are published as papers in journals the summary is often replaced by an abstract. Abstracts follow the title (journal articles do not normally include contents or lists of tables and figures) and state what has been done, why, what was found and what was concluded. Sometimes journals will additionally require key words which are pertinent to the theme of the research. These enable computer key word searches to be facilitated. Abstracts vary in length but rarely exceed 300 words.

### Main text – introduction

This, the first major section of the report, sets the scene and background of the research. Introductory sections identify the need or problem which is to be investigated and comments on how the research relates to other research undertaken in the past. For reports of an academic nature a literature review is a crucial part of the introductory section. The background reading which was carried out, which influenced the style or context of the project, should be referred to. One aspect where literature can support the design of a research project is in the acknowledgement of any limitations. Where other authors have tried and tested certain aspects pertinent to the project, their work can be cited to justify your approach. In essence the introduction builds a picture of what will happen in the rest of the report. It may be useful at the end of the introduction to specify how the remainder of the report is organized. Doing this assists the reader in knowing what to expect and helps them to follow your logic. From this base the next section naturally flows.

## Aims and objectives

While some see a statement of aims and objectives as part of the introduction, it is such an important section that it may well be better to highlight it separately. Out of the introduction, background and literature should come your specific research aims (principal questions to be investigated) and objectives (secondary questions posed to assist in the answer of the project aims). In some reports a section called **Terms of reference** is included as an alternative to the aims, objectives and to a certain extent the introduction. This is more common in consultancy reports where the project aims are specified in the research contract. Thus it is unnecessary for the consultant to write a lengthy introductory section because the client has already stated why the project is to be undertaken. Terms of reference, therefore, relate to a statement of the subject matter of the report, its purpose and who the report is for (the client).

## Methods

All reports include a section on the method(s) used in the research and this follows whatever variation of introductory section(s) are used. To this point you have set the scene in your introduction, referred to other work, acknowledged limitations, stated your aims and objectives and now are ready to say how the work was done. The method section, therefore, explains how the research aims were approached, why particular techniques were used and how they were put into action. For surveys it is necessary to explain aspects of data collection, sampling, respondent selection, questionnaire design, principal methods of analysis and any other features of methodology that are applicable. It may be useful to refer back to the literature for assistance in the justification of your methodology. A feature here (particularly for academic research) should be that another researcher could read this section  and be able to repeat the research. Although precise replication of method is more a feature of natural science research, as a theme to guide the writer in this context it is useful.

## Results

The results sections are at the centre of a report and will vary in length and format in relation to the scope and aims of the project. In the case of a market research report where a survey was involved there needs to be a distinction between a statement or description of the results and any statistical (or other) analysis.

When describing results, care should be given to do just this and not to overlap with the later sections of analysis and interpretation. For example, where a structured questionnaire was used the description of results relates to a statement of the frequencies for each question. Here consideration should be made of how best to illustrate the data. Tables, charts and graphs are often used to guide the reader through the results. It is unnecessary to repeat verbatim all that is shown in a table or chart in any accompanying text. However, salient points should be described additionally in the text. Rather than treat each answer to a question on the questionnaire consecutively, grouping results around a theme within a sub-section is generally worthwhile. The theme of a sub-section could relate back to a specific project objective (or part of one). This way the reader can follow your logic in how you are beginning to satisfy the aims and objectives stated in the earlier section of the report.

When this moves to the analysis of the results, where statistical tests are applied, relation to the project aims and objectives is again advisable as a structure. By reiterating objectives, or in this case hypotheses, this can provide a structure to the section and the reader can follow the purpose of the analysis.

## Discussion

Following the description and analysis of the results, the findings can now be placed in a context and the implications evaluated and discussed. It is worth beginning the discussion section with a restatement of the aims and objectives and then go on to discuss how well the findings from the previous sections answer these research questions. Where any of the objectives have not been fully answered this should be fully acknowledged.

## Recommendations

In some reports it is necessary to make recommendations. In the field of market research this is highly likely because of its applied nature. Recommendations should be brief and precise and must relate to what has been found from the research. Where the research was limited, recommendations for future developments or other projects can be expressed.

## Conclusion

The final section is a brief and straightforward summary of the methods, results and their implications. It should also be stated how well the research satisfied the aims and objectives set. In short it is what you can justifiably conclude from what you have done and what you have found out. Remember that it is a summary and so you should not introduce new ideas.

## References or bibliography

A list of references is all the books, journals and other sources you have 'referred' to in the text. A bibliography includes these and other sources you consulted but did not actually refer to in the report. Which you select is perhaps a matter of choice or may be specifically dictated (as in the case of reports supporting qualifications or journal articles). Two methods of referencing work in the text and the organization of a bibliography or reference list are explained in a following section.

## Appendices

Additional information which is relevant to the research but not included in the report (to keep it uncluttered) can be appended to (put at the end of) the report. This may include a copy of the questionnaire, interview transcripts, coding scheme, interview schedule and any other relevant material. Somewhere in the text each numbered appendix should be referred to so that the reader is aware of its presence and can make a judgement as to whether he/she need refer to the additional information provided.

## Organizing sections

### Numbering

In most reports there is a numbering system applied to each major section, and sometimes also to sub-sections, such as:

>Section 3  Methodology
>     3.1  Sampling
>          3.1.1  Introduction
>          3.1.2  Sampling method
>          3.1.3  Sample selection
>          3.1.4  Sample size
>     3.2  Data collection, etc.

It is recommended that no further subdivisions are used as the numbering system can become too cluttered and may distract the reader. In the example given the major section or chapter is divided first into the main topic areas (sampling, data collection, etc.) and then each of these are subdivided into the discussion of more specific aspects. In some reports where particular references are required, such as government reports, an alternative is to number each paragraph. Unless instructed to do so it is normally unnecessary to go this far.

The pages of a report should be numbered (as shown on the contents page). It is conventional in books for the introduction to begin as page 1, in arabic numbers (1, 2, 3, etc.) and for sections prior to this (acknowledgements, summary, foreword, etc.) to have roman numbers (i, ii, iii, iv, etc.). This is reasonably straightforward if a word processing package is being used. In some reports and with some educational institutions it is a requirement that all pages are numbered consecutively beginning with 1.

With appendices, it may be more difficult to page number because some of the material in them may not have been word processed. While it is essential to number each appendix, the use of page numbers as well varies. It is important, especially where readers are likely to need to refer to the appendices, that page numbers should extend to this section.

*Citation in the text 1: Harvard system*

At every point in the text of a book, essay or report at which a citation (reference to a particular document) is made, it is essential that the source can be identified. One method, called the Harvard system, requires the author's name and the year of publication to be inserted after each reference in the text. If the author's surname occurs naturally in the sentence then only the year is given in brackets, e.g.:

Krippendorf (1987) describes ...

If not, then both author and date are included in parentheses, e.g.:

In an earlier study (Patmore, 1983) it is described as ...

If the author has more than one document published in the same year cited in your work they are identified by adding lower case letters after the year, and within the parentheses, e.g.:

Smith (1992a) discussed the subject ...

or

In a further article (Smith 1992b), it was suggested ...

If there are two authors, the surnames of both should be given before the date. If there are more than two authors, the surname of the first should be given followed by '*et al.*', (this is an abbreviation of 'et alia' which means 'and others'). When citing references in the text you should not include the authors' initials, unless to distinguish between more than one author with the same surname. If no person is named who can be treated as the author, and the title or title page implies that an organization is mainly responsible for the publication, this body may be treated as the author. This may include certain publications by ETB, BTA, etc. On very rare occasions there may be neither author nor organization, and these may be shown by 'Anon.' in place of the authors' name, meaning anonymous.

To further complicate matters, if different parts of a document are cited in different parts of the text, the appropriate page or section number(s) may be given in the text, following the date and within the parentheses, e.g.:

Smith (1992b: 120) describes ...

### Citation in the text 2: The numeric system

With this system, instead of the name and date, a number in the text refers to the origins of any sources used. Numbers are either placed in parentheses or in superscript. If the same source is used more than once in the text then the same number first cited is used in each subsequent citation. A list of references showing the full reference is provided at the end of the report. For example:

> Science and technology are continually providing new means of stretching the limits of the ecosystem (1). This created the illusion that the negative side-effects of economic growth can always be eliminated by modern technology (2).

or

> Science and technology are continually providing new means of stretching the limits of the ecosystem.[1] This created the illusion that the negative side-effects of economic growth can always be eliminated by modern technology.[2]

### Reference lists: Harvard system

Books and reports always give a list of references or a bibliography of the information used by the author in preparing the paper. This allows those reading the work to check the sources and decide for themselves whether the conclusions drawn are valid as well as to find more information on a subject.

The bibliography, which includes references cited in the text together with other sources used but not cited, should be presented as a list at the end of the text. The list should be arranged in alphabetical order of authors' surnames, and then by year and letter, if applicable. References should be produced following the layout given below, sections given in *italics* may be underlined if you are using a typewriter, which cannot produce italic script, or handwritten reports. The way in which a reference is given depends on the nature of the source.

**REFERENCE TO A BOOK OR REPORT**

Author(s). Year of publication. *Title*, Edition number (if relevant). Page or chapter number(s) (if relevant). Place where published: publisher.

e.g.  Harrison, C. (1991). *Countryside recreation in a changing society*. Chapter 4. Bristol: The TMS Partnership.

Similarly a reference to a report should be shown thus:

Countryside Commission, (1985). *National countryside recreation survey 1984*. CCP 201. Cheltenham: Countryside Commission.

**REFERENCE TO A CONTRIBUTION IN A BOOK**

Author(s) of contribution. Year of publication. Title of contribution followed by 'In:'. Editor(s) of book. *Title of book*. Edition number (if relevant), page number(s) of contribution.

e.g.  Hollands, R.G. (1985). 'Working class youth, leisure and the search for work'. In: Parker, S.R. and Veal, A.J. (eds) *Work, non-work and leisure*. London: Leisure Studies Association, 3–29.

**REFERENCE TO A CONTRIBUTION IN A JOURNAL**

When referencing from a journal, follow the same guidelines, but remember to include the volume and issue numbers. This time just to complicate matters instead of writing the title in *italics* the title of the periodical is written in *italics*. So the order for a journal is:

Author(s) of the contribution. Year of publication. Title of the contribution. *Title of the journal*, Volume number, Page number(s).

e.g.  Child, E. (1983). Play and culture: A study of English and Asian Children. *Leisure Studies*, Vol. 2 , No. 2, 169–86.

**REFERENCE TO A CONTRIBUTION IN THE POPULAR PRESS**

This is similar to the way a periodical is referenced with the exception that because publications in the popular press rarely have volume numbers, the date of the publication is inserted in its place.

e.g. Waters, R. (1991). Flawed financial structure was International Leisure Group's undoing. *Financial Times.* March 16th 1991, 6.

**THE USE OF PERSONAL COMMUNICATIONS**

Sometimes your source will be a conversation, lecture notes or other unpublished information. In this case you write:

e.g.  Major, J. (1992). Personal communication.

*Reference lists: numeric system*

All sources referred to in the numeric system are similarly listed at the end of the main text of a report. Here however, entries are arranged in numerical order as opposed to alphabetical order as with the previous system. Following the number, the organization of the reference is as for the Harvard system. For example:

1    Krippendorf, J. (1987). *The Holidaymakers.* Oxford: Butterworth-Heinemann.
2    Strassenliga, D. and Gesellschaft, D. (eds.) (1980). *Freizeit und Ssrasse: Aktive freizeitgestaltung und verkehr.* Koln: Druckhaus Muller.

**Other aspects of report writing**

*Getting in the mood for writing*

Writing reports is not particularly easy and every writer has moments when things seem to fall into place and other times when nothing seems to go well and writing anything is an uphill struggle. For some, the approaching deadline helps and they can 'burn the midnight oil' but this is a risky strategy especially if you are likely to fall asleep. You must work out what strategy works best for you and plan around this. It can be particularly difficult if many other work commitments occur at the same time as you are trying to write your report. This is because it is easy to deal with minor things and leave writing (which is more difficult) aside. Ideally you should plan ahead and make some space where you can concentrate on the writing. This is because you need time to think as well as write, so allowing yourself the odd hour before lunch (or before going out) is unlikely to be very successful. Other aspects which you may find useful are listed below.

## 1 PLANNING

Plan a whole section in advance and think about how the sub-sections fit into it. Then give yourself deadlines for completing each part. This way you can monitor your own progress.

## 2 ROUTINE

Try and get into a routine of writing something each day, so you feel as if you are progressing and getting nearer the end. Once a section is planned, write it up as soon as possible so that you remember what you intended.

## 3 THE FLOW

Sometimes when things go well and your ideas are flowing onto the page, capitalize on it. Do not stop to check a reference or design a table, keep going. Checking and minor jobs can be done later. Remember some sections (results and discussion) are better written in one go rather than broken down over a longer time period, so plan for this if you can.

## 4 STOPPING FOR A BREAK

When you stop writing, think about where you are going to start the next time. If you have come to an abrupt halt because of a difficult section, try and make a few inroads into it before you stop. Otherwise the thought of starting again may be much harder.

## 5 WORKPLACE

Find a place to work where there are few distractions and where it is quiet. You may need to tell others what you are doing and ask not to be disturbed. If there are lots of things going on around you, it may be more difficult to get into a rhythm of writing.

## 6  DRAFTING

You are highly unlikely to have everything perfect in a first draft. Several drafts may be needed, so you should allow time for this in your plans. Once a section has been written as a first draft, some writers find it worthwhile to put it to one side and do other jobs, returning to it later with a fresh mind to check to see if it makes sense and make amendments.

## 7  GET HELP

Ask a colleague to look over your work to see if what you have written is easily understood. If possible ask someone who has not been closely associated with your research. This way they can better comment on whether your explanations can be followed than somebody who already has a fair idea of what you are trying to say.

## 8  REWARD

Reward yourself for a job well done. Whether this is a celebratory drink or a sticky bun at the end of a busy afternoon, take time out and treat yourself. Giving yourself treats when you have achieved your own deadlines or targets can help with your own motivation – you deserve it after all.

### *Is it any good?*

Before beginning the final draft you should look back over the whole report with a critical eye. The following questions may help you as a guide, but others, specific to your project will need to be added.

1  Title and introductory sections
   - Is the title relevant?
   - Does the introduction set the scene?
   - Are the aims and objectives clearly stated?
   - Is the summary fair and concise?
   - Have all the sources in the literature review been properly recorded?
   - Are the reasons for the project clear?

2  Main sections
   - Are the sections clearly presented?
   - Are the sections in a logical sequence?
   - Is your report easy to follow (for example are the aims and objectives developed as consistent themes)?
   - Are all tables, figures, appendices and references labelled and referred to properly?
   - Is your conclusion brief, related to the main findings and to the purpose of the research?

3  Paragraphs
   - Are paragraphs complete mini-topics in themselves?
   - Do they start with an appropriate topic sentence?
   - Do they contain information relating only to the paragraph topic?
   - Do the paragraphs link the section together?

4  Writing clearly
   - Do your ideas emerge clearly?
   - Will your language be understood by the readership?
   - Are sentences too long?
   - Have the spelling and punctuation been checked (do this after the final draft too)?
   - Are certain words repeated too often?
   - Have you been consistent in the tense you have used?

5  Layout
   - Is the layout appropriate for the readership/instructions given?
   - Has a consistent system been used for headings and section numbering?
   - Is the contents page still accurate?
   - Is the style of font, size and printing finish clear and easy to read?

## 8.3  Giving presentations

### Introduction

A presentation is a form of communication where a speaker talks on a given subject to an audience. There is a wide variety of different types of presentation within this definition, from an employee reporting back the interim findings of a research project for colleagues at a meeting, to the after dinner speech or conference presentation. Here the audience could be several hundred. Whatever the nature, there are some basic guidelines which are important to recognize and this section investigates some of the main issues. The focus for this section is for a presentation in between these two extremes. That is where there is a greater need for planning than when giving a verbal report to a meeting but some way short of a theatrical performance.

## Planning – first thoughts

### 1 The purpose

Throughout this text the theme of returning to your aims and objectives has been a constantly recurring one. Giving a presentation is no exception. The first question should be to determine the purpose of the presentation and to develop a specific aim and objectives for it. This could be in the form of a particular title, question or recommendation such as 'to explain how our market research findings can inform the company strategy'. Even this may be too general, but whatever the aim of the presentation it should remain as a focus for the whole planning procedure.

### 2 Who is the audience?

Closely bound with the first point, what you aim to talk about, is to consider who is going to be listening. This will influence the later stages of the planning process in terms of the content of the presentation, its length, and the use of visual aids. To a small technical audience of fellow researchers their knowledge of your research and its methods may be high compared to a large general audience or one which is mixed. Whatever your circumstances you should ask the following questions:

- What does the audience already know about my subject?
- What are they coming to learn, or what interests them?
- What are their feelings (or prejudices) likely to be about my subject?
- Do they all feel/think/know the same?
- What resistance are they likely to have towards me or my subject?

- What is the likely size of the audience?

Keeping in mind both what you aim to present while being sensitive to the type of audience will help establish the emphasis of the remaining preparatory stages.

### 3 The major topics and the structure

This stage involves identifying the major topics which will form the principal content of the presentation. Obviously this is determined by the subject of the presentation, however there are three aspects you should be mindful of. First, how can each major topic be divided into more manageable sections? Second, how large are these sections? If possible, each major topic and the sections within it should be of equal length. For example, if there are two major topics and each is divided into three sections, making six in total, all six should be roughly similar in duration. Third, consider a logical sequence for the sections. In doing this you should always be aware of how you will be able to relate each section back to the major topic and of course back to the aim of the presentation.

### 4 Content and length

The amount of time given to you for the presentation may well have been decided in advance and once known it is necessary to think carefully about how much you have to say. You will have already identified the sections and put them in a sequence; now you can actually write down the contents of each section while being mindful of how long you will have to speak. It is worthwhile at this point attaching a ranking system of priority to each section. This will help if later it becomes clear that the presentation will be over-length and you must make some cuts. Do not worry too much about writing the finished version (see Section 8.2) but aim to be short. This will allow you time to speak of 'signposts', reminders of where you are in the structure of the presentation. Remember that an audience is quickly irritated by a presentation which overruns into the coffee or lunch break, but few are similarly irritated by a good presentation which is a little short.

## 5 *How to start*

When beginning a presentation the initial moments are quite crucial. The audience must accept you as the speaker and feel comfortable with you. Some people are naturally humorous and confident enough to begin with a joke. This can work well, but if the joke is unrelated, not funny or in some way inappropriate, it can ruin the whole presentation. With large unfamiliar audiences this strategy is particularly treacherous. A safer alternative is to express how pleased you are to be there and to have the opportunity to speak. In other words you are not presenting yourself as the best orator the audience will ever come across, rather you are an interesting, hard-working person, like themselves, who is worthwhile listening to.

Explaining the layout/structure of your talk is also crucial. You should start with what you are going to talk about in general terms and how you are going to divide the subject into sections. Essentially you are establishing the signposts, previously referred to, so the audience will know where they are at any time during the presentation. For instance, if they know that you are talking on the fifth of six sections (which have each lasted about five minutes) and their empty stomach starts to rumble, they have an idea about how long they have to wait before lunch.

## 6 *Relating to the audience*

Every so often it will be necessary to reflect on how the audience is coping with the subject of your talk. You should have frequent summaries where you clarify where you have come from and what must still be done to satisfy the aim of the presentation. This helps the audience to follow your logic or line of argument. Presentations which are a string of facts or technical terms become progressively more difficult to follow unless the audience is repeatedly reminded of the structure and purpose.

## 7 *Tell them a story*

When writing a presentation, if you believe that it will be difficult to develop a logical sequence consider telling a story. Very factual information can be made more interesting if you explain how you went about doing the investigation. For example, 'the data collection method, focus groups, gave us problems selecting the right people to take part ... first we tried ... then when this didn't work in the pilot we ... then we found we couldn't ... so finally we managed to ...'

When making a presentation you should be talking to an audience and not reading to them. If a written report accompanies your presentation, then the interested members of the audience can read this on their own. A presentation and a written report are different tools of communication, the former could motivate an individual to read the latter. However, a presentation quickly becomes boring if basically all you are doing is reading out your report. Hence, developing a storyline can go a long way in making rather plain research findings into something which is pleasant to listen to and easy to follow.

## Planning – second thoughts

Having decided what to include in a presentation, reflected on the type of audience, decided what are the main topics and sections, given them an order, written down what is involved while being mindful of how long you will have to speak, signposted where necessary and decided on a narrative style, are you ready to go? Possibly, but there are some other aspects worth contemplating.

### 1 The attention curve of the audience

It is well known that for a presentation of, say, 45 minutes, the attention span of the audience drops sharply after 10 minutes, continues to fall and rises for the last 5 minutes or so. To overcome this to a certain extent, dividing the presentation into smaller manageable parts helps. However, even the best speaker realizes how an audience loses attention and makes his/her important points at the beginning and end of a presentation. Moreover, knowing that the audience starts to lose attention after ten minutes can help to inform you of when to show slides or use other visual aids. Changes in the style of delivery can also assist in the revival of sagging attention.

### 2 Take a break

Having a break rarely annoys anybody. If you have structured your presentation as outlined here, then there should be natural points where a break can occur. It is probably better to have more shorter breaks than a single long one. If, however, you are committed to having a single break part way through your presentation it may be better to have it a little way past the half-way point. That way the audience knows that they have less to come back to than before the break (assuming you keep to time). You should clearly signpost where breaks are to occur and remind the audience of what is to be done after the break. Remember that a break means getting up, moving around or having a coffee, and does not mean pausing in your talk to ask if there are any questions.

### 3 Audience participation

The type of presentation which is envisaged here is unlikely to involve splitting the audience into smaller groups and sending them away to complete a particular task. With very large audiences participation is difficult; however, with smaller ones the passing round of brochures or other physical objects may be worthwhile. The main form of participation comes in the form of questions. As the presenter you should take the lead in inviting questions at suitable points in the presentation. Assuming you have used up all your allotted time, it is unlikely that asking questions at the end, as an afterthought, will result in anything fruitful being asked. It is better to be specific and ask for questions at the end of a particular topic to see if further clarification is necessary. With this in mind, there may be certain scenarios which arise when you ask, 'are there any questions concerning ...'.

a  **Silence:** This can feel quite awkward, but you should allow a sufficient pause, which may feel like an eternity, before proceeding.

b  **The question which helps:** This is a question from the audience which seeks relevant clarification. This type should be welcomed and answered immediately.

c  **The irrelevant question:** This type of question is so specific or technical that you sense that the majority of the audience are uninterested or that to answer it would take too long. In this case indicate that to properly answer the question would take too long but that you would be happy to discuss the matter with the questioner and anyone else interested at the next break.

d  **The awkward questioner:** Occasionally questions are asked which are deliberately off-putting. It is not recommended that you enter into an exchange with somebody out to damage you.

In a similar way to type (c), offer to answer the question individually and informally following the presentation.

It may be every presenter's nightmare to have somebody in the audience out to make you appear stupid. It is also very annoying to you, however you must appear absolutely reasonable and unruffled. If you anticipate that this type of questioner may be in your audience, prepare an answer in advance. You could say, 'I will need more time to properly consider such an interesting question, perhaps we could meet informally before lunch and discuss things fully. Now returning to the next section ...'. In short you have put the questioner down politely, but have not entered into an exchange (in not seeking a response to your invitation of a discussion before lunch). In this prepared answer you have taken the lead, indicated how and when you will answer and then immediately get on with the presentation.

## 4 Using a script

It is difficult to know how much of the content of a presentation needs to be written down in advance and used in the presentation. There are two extremes: giving a spontaneous presentation without notes or visual aids, and reading out loud a written paper. The former is extremely dangerous and risks going either over length, quickly running out of things to say, or forgetting a memorized speech. The latter can be very tedious, and some would say insulting, to listen to. The most interesting style of delivery is where somebody appears to be talking to you, but mimicking this is not easy. When writing your presentation you should write it as you would speak not as you would write a research paper. Probably the best way to do this is to think, when writing, how you would say something if explaining it to another and transcribing this. It is also a good idea to continually practise reading out what you have just written.

When it comes towards a final version you may find that you have almost memorized what you have written. The question then is to decide how much written material you will need with you when giving the presentation. Having a whole script enhances the likelihood that you will end up reading it, which is what you are trying to avoid. You should be able to condense a script down to sections with key words and phrases to prompt you. Placing these onto cards is a good idea.

In short, the process of developing the actual script involves first writing it out in full using spoken rather than written English.

Second, reciting this and refining as necessary, and finally placing what you need onto cards to guide you during the delivery.

### 5 *Your mannerisms*

Nobody likes their particular mannerisms pointed out to them, but occasionally nerves make us do things which would be distracting when giving a presentation. It is worthwhile, particularly for the beginner, to have oneself videotaped or watched by others who are looking for just such distractions. The most common of these include:

a **Physical distractions:** Repeatedly moving around, scratching your nose, constantly adjusting a transparency, etc.
b **Verbal distractions:** Repeatedly using the same word or phrase, such as 'basically', 'actually', 'the thing is', 'you know'.
c **Eye contact:** Maintaining eye contact with the audience is important. Head down reading notes is distracting, but a fixed head on the back of the room can be equally so.
d **Speed:** Often presenters speak far too quickly. Remember that the content is very familiar to you but will not be to the audience. They will need time to understand it.
e **Pitch:** Some speak too loud and others too quietly. Others have the correct pitch most of the time but drop it towards the end of a sentence. Practice and being aware of this aspect help.

## Visual aids

Using some sort of visual aid to support a presentation is common practice but, as with other areas of presentation, there are also some pitfalls. At a general level you should be aware of the following guidelines:

1 **Relevance:** The visual aids used should be clearly linked to the purpose of the presentation or the point you are trying to make and should be appropriate in terms of the level of understanding of your audience.
2 **Simple:** Visual aids must get straight to the point. If you have to spend too much time explaining what is shown, the purpose and value of them can be quickly lost.
3 **Emphasis:** You must use your visual aids to emphasize a particular point, stress an important idea, indicate a change in

the structure or identify a new concept. They are there to ease understanding.

4 **Consistency:** It is better to develop a consistent style in your visual aids. Constant changing from one type to another can be confusing.

Some of the main types of visual aids include:

### 1 *The overhead projector*

The overhead projector (OHP) is a useful tool in that it can project a wide range of written and diagrammatic information. In using an OHP you can point to particular parts of an acetate without turning your back on the audience. Acetates can be prepared in advance and overlays are particularly helpful to build an idea as the presentation progresses. Lettering on an acetate, where it is handwritten, should be as large as possible (and not less than about 10mm) and bold colours such as black, brown, blue and green are often easier to see at a distance than light colours such as red, orange or yellow.

Word processed information can often be put directly onto acetates or photocopied onto suitable acetate film which can withstand the heat of the photocopier. Again the lettering should be much larger than normal type. It is possible to use attachments to computers to display the screen directly through an adapted OHP. If a presentation is to be repeated several times, it may be worth going to the trouble of learning how to use the presentation software. However, such equipment often requires a darkened room, so you should ensure that this is available.

Whether you are using an OHP as a whiteboard to write on key words while the presentation progresses, or using prepared acetates, there are some guidelines:

a Ensure that the OHP you will be using is sufficiently powerful for the room you will be using and that the room can be darkened if necessary.

b Have one main idea for each acetate. Having several simple acetates is much better than a single complicated one.

c If you are photocopying original typewritten material onto acetate it will need to be enlarged. Similarly handwritten ones should be in large writing.

d Practise beforehand, and become proficient in positioning and focussing the OHP.

e Use card instead of paper to mask off aspects of an acetate which you want to gradually reveal. Card, being heavier, is less likely to fall off.

f Give your audience time to read or look at your overheads. This may mean that you stop talking while the audience takes it all in.

g Turn the OHP off when you have finished explaining an acetate. When the relevance of an overhead has passed, its continued projection can become distracting.

### 2 Whiteboards and flipcharts

These are often used to highlight particular points as the presentation progresses, though sometimes they are prepared in advance. It is important to remember that felt pens used on whiteboards can also be used on flipcharts but the same is not true in reverse. Whiteboard markers which can be removed with a dry cloth must be used if you wish to use the board more than once in a presentation. When using whiteboards or flipcharts the following guidelines may be useful:

a Start with a clean board or page.

b Avoid talking to the board when you are writing. Pausing briefly while you write will not stop the attention of the audience.

c Take your time, write clearly in large letters.

d Pause and stand clear of the board when you have finished so that your audience can see what you have written and take it in.

e Use bold colours, following the same rule as for overheads (yellow, red and orange can be more difficult to see).

f If possible practise beforehand, and see if what you write can be read from the back of the room.

### 3 Slide projectors

Similar rules apply for slide projectors as for the OHP but you must ensure that the room can be sufficiently darkened. This may mean that notetaking cannot occur, which you should recognize and account for. As with acetates, each slide must be relevant and simple with any written information easily read. Again, once discussed, the projector should be turned off rather than an old slide being left on as a distraction.

It is vitally important that you know how to use the slide projector as they can jam. Numbered slides must be placed in the projector the right way up and in order. If a projectionist is available to assist you, he/she should be clearly briefed of the purpose and structure of your presentation and when he/she will be needed. With some projectors a light pen with a projected arrow is supplied. Only use this if absolutely necessary, as it can be distracting when a fairy-like image dances around the room as you fiddle to try and get it to point at something.

There is perhaps more room for error with slides than with acetates or whiteboards. Practice and a quick run through are important. However supportive your audience is, if your first slide jams, your second is out of order, and your third is upside down, you may not be heard above the laughter.

### 4 Video and film

A good video or film as part of a presentation can be a great success but, as with slides, the more complicated your visual aids become, the more room there is for error. The following suggestions may help.

a Do not make the film too long, otherwise it may take over the presentation.

b Only use film or video if it is relevant, simple and helps emphasize a suitable point.

c Consider carefully when, during the presentation, it is best to show the film.

d Take care in making additional comments during a film. With any type of sound film you probably will not be heard by everybody. With a silent film, rehearsal is vital, so that your comments match the appropriate point in the film and also finish in the right place.

e Video filming requires training, doing it yourself is dangerous. It can easily look like a home movie and the audience can quickly become more aware of its shortcomings than of the message you are trying to give.

f Do not perform in it. However much you may have liked to have been a television presenter, doing so well requires skill and training. Most film commentaries performed by untrained presenters have a habit of appearing like something from a Monty Python sketch. If you do appear in a film, get an honest opinion from a trusted colleague before you decide to use it.

Perhaps the main questions to ask yourself when thinking of using a video or film are:

- Why is this video being substituted for me in the presentation?
- Is a video or film an appropriate technique to achieve my aims?

## Summary

This chapter has attempted to provide some useful guidelines when writing a report or giving a presentation. To summarize, three key points should be remembered (after Walters, 1993):

1 Have a purpose, so that you know exactly what you want to achieve and pass on to your reader or audience.
2 Realise that your reader or audience will not remember everything you have said or written. Identify three or four key ideas that must be remembered and that they can take away with them.
3 With presentations, speak with enthusiasm for your topic and consideration for your audience.

## Exercises

1 Select journals from different disciplines and contrast the different approaches to the writing of articles.
2 Using reports produced by the British Tourist Authority or English Tourist Board, where surveys have been used, identify how the authors have divided the information into major and minor sections. How are they numbered?
3 Prepare a short presentation (ten minutes' duration) on how to correctly cite authors when writing reports and how to prepare a reference list. If possible, try out the presentation within a group. Other topics could include how to number sections in a report, writing the first draft, and the do's and don'ts of giving a presentation.

# Further reading

Bell, J. (1993). *Doing your research project*. Second edition. Buckingham: Open University Press.

A very useful reference book for the first-time student through to those undertaking a higher degree. There are valuable ideas from initial project preparation through data collection to writing the report.


Berry, R. (1994). *The research project: How to write it*. London: Routledge.

This book was developed from an original work called 'How to write a research paper' written by the same author in 1966. Its emphasis is for research reports of a more academic rather than consultancy nature. The book is concisely written with sections on choosing a topic, using the library, making notes, comparing and developing the text and how to avoid some common errors.


Walters, L. (1993). *Secrets of successful speakers*. New York: McGraw-Hill.

Covers 11 steps to giving successful speeches and presentations. These include setting objectives, considering the audience, conquering fear, being credible, developing a theme, organizing material, motivating an audience and how to avoid some of the common pitfalls.

# Glossary

**Bias** – The differences between the values derived from a sample survey and the true values for the whole population.

**Cardinal data** – Data which can be given a numerical value, such as age, weight, etc. Sometimes referred to as numerical data.

**Categorical data** – Data which have been put into categories/ classes (e.g. age groups), sometimes referred to as nominal data.

**Cell** – The count or a value in one section of a table.

**Chi-square** – Test used to find out whether two variables are associated.

**Closed question** – A question with a limited number of pre-defined answers (e.g. tick-a-box, score, rank, etc.)

**Coding** – The process of assigning a numerical value to all the data collected in the survey and recording the data in a form ready for analysis (possibly by computer).

**Contingency (cross-tabulation) table** – Table used to display the frequencies of two or more variables where data are in categorical or nominal form.

**Correlation** – The extent of association between variables.

**Dependent variable** – A variable which is to be explained or predicted, and is dependent on one or more variables which may control or relate to it.

**Expected frequency** – A value in a table cell which relates to the number of cases expected; if the row variable and column variable were independent of each other.

**Filter** – An instruction within the questionnaire indicating which questions the interviewer should ask.

**Household survey** – a survey conducted in the home of the respondent.

**Independent variables** – Variables which explain or predict changes in dependent variables. Often they are aspects such as age, gender, income, etc., over which the respondent has no control.

**Interviewer administered questionnaire** – a questionnaire from which questions are asked of the respondent by an interviewer in a face-to-face interview.

**Level of significance** – The probability level used when rejecting a null hypothesis.

**Mean** – A value relating to the average of the observations in a data set.

**Measures of central tendency** – The mean, median and mode, all values which indicate the centre of a distribution.

**Median** – The value in the middle of a data set which has been ranked.

**Mode** – A value in a data set which occurs most often, i.e. the most popular value.

**Normal distribution** – A distribution which is symmetrical about the mean. When plotted it is a smooth, bell-shaped curve.

**Null hypothesis** – A statement in the form that there is no association in the mean, or other values, obtained by two groups or variables. Statistical significance is said to occur when a null hypothesis is rejected.

**Open question** – A question to which a respondent can give as many replies as he/she wishes.

**Ordinal data** – Data which is put into a rank order, though the order may be arbitrary.

**Percentile** – A value which is equal to or less than on a percentage scale. For example a value of the 20th percentile means that 20 per cent of values in a distribution were same or less than this value.

**Pilot** – A small scale survey preceding the main survey designed to test the survey methods and the techniques used.

**Probe** – Questions asked by an interviewer to encourage the respondent to amplify his/her answers.

**Range** – The difference between the highest and lowest values of a data set.

**Sample** – The individuals in a survey population who are selected to act as representatives of that population in a sample survey.

**Sample survey** – An investigation in which information is collected from only a proportion of the survey population. The sample data collected are often used to make inferences about the whole survey population.

**Sampling unit** – The individual (or unit) in the survey population selected to form the basis of the sample and about which information is collected.

**Self-selected sample** – A sample in which respondents have offered themselves for interview rather than being selected as part of a selection procedure.

**Survey population** – The total number of individuals (or units) about which a survey is designed to collect information (e.g. the survey population could be the population of a country aged 18–65 , all the farmers in a region, or even more specific such as all the National Park Officers).

**Spearman's rank correlation** – Statistical test used to describe the relationship between two variables with ordinal data.

**Standard deviation** – Measure of spread of data about the mean.

**Variable** – The term used to describe each individual item of a data set; e.g. data on the number of visitors at a recreation site, their age, sex, reason for visiting, would each form individual variables in the data set collected by the survey.

# Bibliography

Bailey, K.D. (1987). *Methods of social research*. London: The Free Press.

Bales, R.F. (1950). A set of categories for the analysis of small group interaction. *American Sociological Review*, **15**, 257–263.

Bardon, K.S. and Harding, D.M. (1981). On-site questionnaire surveys in UK leisure research. *Tourism Management*. 36–48.

Barnet, V. (1991). *Sample survey : Principles and methods*. London: Edward Arnold.

Bell, J. (1993). *Doing your research project*. Second edition. Buckingham: Open University Press.

Berg, B.L. (1994). *Qualitative research methods for the social sciences*. Boston: Allyn and Bacon.

Berry, R. (1994). *The research project: How to write it*. London: Routledge.

British Tourist Authority and English Tourist Board (1990). *British Coach Operators survey*. London: BTA/ETB.

British Tourist Authority and English Tourist Board (1992). *British holiday intentions*. London: BTA/ETB.

Brunt, P.R. (1990). Tourism trip decision making at the sub-regional level: with special reference to Southern England. University of Bournemouth: Unpublished PhD thesis.

Brunt, P.R. (1995). Commissioning research. *Tourism Intelligence Quarterly*, **7**, 5, 77–84. London: English Tourist Board.

Bryman, A. and Burgess, R.G. (eds) (1994). *Analyzing Qualitative Data*. London: Routledge.

Central Statistical Office (1995). *Travel trends: A report on the 1994 International Passenger Survey*. London: HMSO.

Cochran, W.G. (1977). *Sampling techniques*. Third edition. New York: Wiley.

Cooper, D.R. and Emory, C.W. (1995). *Business Research methods*. Fifth edition. Homewood, Illinois: Irwin.

Czaja, R. (1995). *Designing a survey: A guide to decisions and procedures*. California: Thousand Oaks.

Economist, The (1992). Don't shoot the pollsters. *The Economist* April 18th 1992. London: Economist Newspapers.

English Tourist Board, Northern Ireland Tourist Board, Scottish Tourist Board and Welsh Tourist Board (1994). *The UK Tourist*. London: ETB.

Fink, A. and Kosecoff, J. (1985). *How to conduct surveys: a step by step guide*. Beverly Hills: Sage Publications.

Fink, A. (1995). *How to analyze survey data*. London: Sage Publications.

Fowler, F.J. (1984). *Survey research methods*. Beverly Hills: Sage Publications.

Fowler, F.J. (1993). *Survey research methods*. Second edition. London: Sage Publications.

Frankfort-Nachmias, C. and Nachmias, D. (1992). *Research methods in the social sciences*. Fourth edition. London: Edward Arnold.

Frey, J.H. 1990. *Survey research by telephone*. Second edition. Beverly Hills: Sage Publications.

Frey, J.H. and Oishi, S.M. (1995). *How to conduct interviews by telephone and in person*. London: Sage Publications.

Gardner, G. (1978). *Social surveys for social planners*. Milton Keynes: The Open University Press.

Gill, J. and Johnson, P. (1991). *Research methods for managers*. London: Paul Chapman Publishing.

Groves, R.M. (1989). *Survey errors and survey costs*. New York: Wiley.

Hague, P. (1993). *Questionnaire design*. London: Kogan Page.

Hedrick, T.E., Bickman, L. and Rog, D.J. (1993). *Applied research design: A practical guide*. London: Sage Publications.

Hoinville, G. and Jowell, R. (1978). *Survey research practice*. London: Heinemann Educational Books.

Holloway, J.C. and Plant, R.V. (1988). *Marketing for tourism*. London: Pitman.

Krippendorf, J. (1987). *The Holidaymakers*. Oxford: Butterworth-Heinemann.

Krueger, R.A. (1994). *Focus groups.* Second edition. London: Sage Publications..

Lang, G. (1994). *A practical guide to research methods.* Lanham: University Press of America.

Lavrakas, P.J. (1993). *Telephone survey methods: Sampling, selection and supervision.* Second edition. London: Sage Publications.

Livingstone, J.M. (1977). *A management guide to market research.* London: Macmillan.

Middleton, V.T.C. (1994). *Marketing in travel and tourism.* Oxford: Butterworth-Heinemann.

Morse, J.M. (Ed.) (1994). *Critical issues in qualitative research methods.* London: Sage Publications.

Moser, C.A. (1958). *Survey methods in social investigation.* London: Heinemann.

Moser, Sir C.A. and Kalton, G. (1993). *Survey methods in social investigation.* Second edition. London: Heinemann.

Nachmias C. and Nachmias, D. (1981). *Research methods in the social sciences.* Second edition. London: Edward Arnold.

Norusis, M.J. (1990). *The SPSS Guide to Data Analysis.* Chicago: SPSS Inc.

Office of Population Censuses and Surveys (1991). *Leisure day visits in Great Britain 1988/89.* London: HMSO Publications.

Office of Population Censuses and Surveys (1995). *General Household Survey 1993.* London: HMSO Publications.

Oppenheim, A.N. (1966). *Questionnaire design and attitude measurement.* London: Heinemann.

Oppenheim, A.N. (1992). *Questionnaire design and attitude measurement.* Second edition. London: Heinemann.

Organisation for Economic Co-operation and Development (1989). *National and international tourism statistics.* Paris: OECD.

Organisation for Economic Co-operation and Development (Annual) *Tourism policy and international tourism,* in OECD member countries. Paris: OECD.

Psathas, G. (1995). *Conversation analysis: The study of talk-in-interaction.* London: Sage Publications.

Ritchie, J. and Spencer, L. (1994). Qualitative data analysis for applied policy research. In, Bryman, A. and Burgess, R.G. (eds). *Analyzing Qualitative Data.* London: Routledge.

Ryan, C. (1995). *Researching tourist satisfaction.* London: Routledge.

Sayer, A. (1992). *Method in Social Science.* London: Routledge.

Schutt, R.K. (1995). *Investigating the social world: The process and practice of research*. California: Thousand Oaks.

Slater, R. and Ascroft, P. (1990). *Quantitative techniques in a business context*. London: Chapman and Hall.

Sekaran, U. (1992). *Research methods for business: A skill building approach*. New York: Wiley.

Smith, S.L.J. (1989). *Tourism analysis: A handbook*. Harlow: Longman Scientific and Technical.

Stewart, D.W. and Kamins, M.A. (1993). *Secondary research: Information, sources and methods*. Second edition. London: Sage Publications.

Strauss, A. and Corbin, J. (1990). *Basics of qualitative research*. London: Sage Publications.

Thomas, J. (1993). *Doing critical ethnography*. London: Sage Publications.

Tourism and Recreation Research Unit, (1983). *Recreation site survey manual: methods and techniques for conducting visitor surveys*. London: University of Edinburgh, E and F.N. Spon.

Veal, A.J. (1992). *Research methods for leisure and tourism: A practical guide*. London: Longman/ Institute of Leisure and Amenity Management.

Walters, L. (1993). *Secrets of successful speakers*. New York: McGraw-Hill.

Webb, S. and Webb, B. (1932). *Methods of social study*. London: Longman.

Yin, R.K. (1993). *Applications of case study research*. London: Sage Publications.

Young, P. (1966). *Scientific social surveys and research*. London: Prentice Hall.

Zikmund, W.G. (1994). *Business research methods*. Fourth edition. Orlando: Dryden Press.

# Index